The American Fiddle Method

VOLUME 1 — FIDDLE
Beginning Tunes and Techniques

Here's your play-along audio contents!

Look it up and download

www.melbay.com/99471BCDEB

1	Boil 'em Cabbage Down [3:23]	9	Old Joe Clark [3:18]	17	Red Wing [3:24]
2	Shortnin' Bread [3:07]	10	Soldier's Joy [2:02]	18	Cairo [2:45]
3	Cripple Creek [2:22]	11	Arran Boat Song [2:03]	19	Turkey in the Straw [3:01]
4	Camptown Races [2:22]	12	Bonaparte's Retreat [1:10]	20	Grandfather's Clock [2:46]
5	Angelina Baker [5:16]	13	Country Waltz [2:24]	21	Wise Old Friend [2:41]
6	Buffalo Gals [2:37]	14	Red Haired Boy [2:12]	22	Stinky's Blues [1:44]
7	Cindy [2:31]	15	Girl I Left Behind Me [3:31]		
8	Crawdad Song [3:24]	16	Southwind [2:35]		

3 4 5 6 7 8 9 0

GRANGER MUSIC PUBLICATIONS, INC.
COPYRIGHT © 1998 BY BRIAN WICKLUND
REISSUED 2005, 2001 BY MEL BAY PUBLICATIONS, INC. (EXCLUSIVE SALES AGENT), PACIFIC, MO 63069.
ALL RIGHTS RESERVED. INTERNATIONAL COPYRIGHT SECURED. B.M.I. MADE AND PRINTED IN U.S.A.
No part of this publication may be reproduced in whole or in part, or stored in a retrieval system, or transmitted in any form
or by any means, electronic, mechanical, photocopy, recording, or otherwise, without written permission of the publisher.

Visit us on the Web at www.melbay.com — E-mail us at email@melbay.com

About the Author

When Brian Wicklund was seven years old, his mother thought he should take Suzuki violin lessons. He was surprised to find out that he liked it. When he heard fiddle music for the first time as a third-grader, however, he really flipped out. Brian practiced hard and got to be pretty good. As a pimply teen, he won a bunch of fiddle contests and played fiddle, mandolin and guitar in a number of bluegrass bands. After graduating from Gustavus Adolphus College with a degree in elementary education, Brian realized that school teachers have to get up pretty early in the morning and so he joined the internationally known bluegrass band Stoney Lonesome and played with them for seven years. Brian currently keeps a busy schedule teaching lessons and workshops. He is a sought-after studio musician and regularly performs with an array of bluegrass, country, and swing ensembles. The Minnesota State Arts Board awarded him a fellowship grant. His recordings have been given wide critical acclaim. Find out about Brian's recordings, performances and workshops at **www.fiddlepal.com**.

Acknowledgments

I am grateful to the many people without whom this series would never have been completed. Robert Hurt, Nina Westbrook, Adam Granger, Tom Schaefer, Ken Sherman, Paul Christianson, Bob Walser and Faith Farr offered invaluable feedback and suggestions. Thanks to Brian Barber for his amazing artwork and insight.

I thank my parents Dave and Faith Wicklund, and Rod and Barb Anderson. I thank my wife Cynthia and my children Clara, Sofie and Ben for their constant support and encouragement and singing on the CD. I would especially like to thank my students for their patience, humor and energy. Finally, I am grateful to the many fine musicians who, through the years, took time to offer me encouragement or show me a lick or two.

About the Illustrator

Brian Barber is pretty tall and has been illustrating and designing for many publications and advertising in Minneapolis since 1989. He moved to Minneapolis from Nebraska, where he attended the University of Nebraska-Lincoln. His musical experience includes playing drums and guitar in several rock and roll bands. His only previous experience with the fiddle is when he was fighting with his sister as a kid and broke her violin bow, and got in really big trouble. Brian's other illustrations are at *www.brianbarber.com.*

Foreword

I was ten years old when I first heard a recording of Paul Warren playing "Foggy Mountain Breakdown" with Lester Flatt and Earl Scruggs. That recording changed my life. I sought out fiddlers, practiced hard, traveled to fiddle contests, joined bands, and ultimately chose music as a career. It is a creative outlet that will forever challenge and interest me. Through music, I have met and become friends with many great people who have exposed me to new music and ideas. I can't imagine my life without it. I still get chills when I hear that old recording.

When I began teaching fiddle lessons, I realized there was a need for a quality, comprehensive program for learning fiddle music. After nine years of revisions based on feedback from students and fellow teachers, I have created *The American Fiddle Method*.

Readers will be led through a basic repertoire of tunes and skills that are common to fiddle players across the United States. Those tunes and skills will be presented in a step-by-step approach with each new skill building on earlier skills.

I have also taken great care to present each tune in what I believe to be its basic melody in its most common key. Because fiddle music is an oral tradition and the melodies are subject to change from one generation to the next or from one part of the country to another, one may hear a wide variety of interpretations of a tune. One who learns the melodies in this series should have no problem playing with folk musicians anywhere.

This method also encourages creativity in the student by including variations to the tunes and showing how they can lead to improvisation. I hope to encourage readers to come up with their own way of playing the music by mixing the variations for the tunes into their own versions.

I personally get the most enjoyment from playing music when "jamming" with others. To help students develop ensemble skills, I have included chords and lyrics to the songs, instruction on basic music theory, and demonstrations of skills such as backup and lead playing on the recording. The *American Fiddle Method* books for cello, viola, piano, and mandolin were written so that all of the tunes are in the same keys, use the same chords, and have compatible versions and variations. Cellists, violists, pianists, mandolin players, and fiddlers will all be able to jam together.

While writing this method, I collaborated with teachers of classical music to fit this fiddle program with their classical violin programs. They have found fiddle tunes and techniques to be a valuable aid in reinforcing their instruction and re-energizing their students' motivation. These tunes are really exciting to play in a heterogeneous school orchestra class.

I have tried to write this book in a style that is easy to understand for both adults and kids, and to employ playful yet informative artwork. I want this book to be fun to look at and read instead of being another dull lesson book.

Finally, I felt it was important to include a listening/play-along recording that captured the excitement of the music. Students will enjoy listening and playing and singing along with the fine musicians on this recording.

See you jamming 'round the campfire at the next festival!

Brian Wicklund

Table of Contents

Foreword 4
How to Become a Great Fiddler 6
The Parts of a Fiddle 7
Bow and Fiddle Position 8
Fingering Position 10
The Anatomy of a Fiddle Tune 12
Potato Introductions 13
Endings 14
Beginning Tunes
    1 Boil 'em Cabbage Down 15
    2 Shortnin' Bread 16
    3 Cripple Creek 17
    4 Camptown Races 18
    5 Angelina Baker 19
    6 Buffalo Gals 20

The Fourth Finger 21
    7 Cindy 22
    8 Crawdad Song 23

The Low Second Finger 24
    9 Old Joe Clark 26
    10 Soldier's Joy 27
    11 Arran Boat Song 28

Down-Driven Bowing and Corrective Slurs 29
    12 Bonaparte's Retreat 31
    13 Country Waltz 31
    14 Red Haired Boy 32
    15 Girl I Left Behind Me 33
    16 Southwind 34

Bow Reset & Staccato Slurs 35
    17 Red Wing 36
    18 Cairo 37
    19 Turkey in the Straw 38

The High Third Finger 39
    20 Grandfather's Clock 40
    21 Wise Old Friend 41
    22 Stinky's Blues 42

Creating Your Own Variations 44
Drone and Double-Stop Variations 44
Slide Variations 50
Beginning Backup Fiddle Playing 53
Review Chart 58
    For the Ensemble Teacher 59
    A Guide to Bluegrass Style Arranging 61

How to Become a Great Fiddler

1. Listen to the recording for this book. Listening to the recording will familiarize you with the melodies, good intonation, tone and style of the music. Listen anytime: while you eat, when you are riding in the car, or as you go to sleep at night. The more you listen, the faster and easier it will be to learn the tunes. Listen to as many other fiddle recordings as you can, too.

2. Practice regularly. Practice four to seven times a week, between 30 minutes and two hours (15 minutes for very young children). For the first portion of your practice work on new material, then review the tunes you already know by playing along with the recording. You can be the only fiddle in the band by turning off the fiddle in the recording using the stereo's balance knob. It's big fun!

Make sessions the same time and place every day to establish a habit. Some people like to keep track of their practices on a calendar and then give themselves a reward for a certain number of practices. I suggest a reward such as a new fiddle recording or tickets to a concert.

3. Practice smart. This element of practice is often overlooked! You can learn skills much faster if you understand the basic principles of learning and memory.

There are two levels of knowing how to play a tune: **melodic memory** and **muscle memory**. After repeatedly listening to the CD, you will be able to hum the tunes and probably pick out the notes on your fiddle with or without the notation. You will be able to hear what the next note should sound like before you play it. This is an important first step in learning the tune. However, in order to be able to play the tune at jamming tempo without making mistakes, you need to take the next step of committing the tune to muscle memory.

When you have done a skill enough times, your brain and muscles get used to that skill and it becomes a habit. Muscle memory allows us to do a skill automatically without having to concentrate on its every single detail. That's why we can walk and talk at the same time, bounce a basketball while thinking about our next move or play a tune at break-neck speed while concentrating on playing expressively. Good players are not just satisfied with their brains knowing how a tune goes; they make sure their muscles know too!

Because your muscles "learn" whatever actions they repeat, it is very important to be sure that you are learning the music correctly and that you are using good position, tone and intonation. Your muscles learn an incorrect skill as readily as a correct one, so make sure you are repeating exactly what you want your muscles to memorize. Everybody knows how difficult it is to change a bad habit!

When learning a new tune, follow these steps:
1. After you have listened to the CD, pick through the melody, either by ear or by reading the notation.
2. Slowly play a small part of the beginning of the tune. If you make a mistake, remember the note that came *before* the mistake.
3. Play the phrase again and pause on the note before your mistake, think about the correct note that comes next and play it.
4. Repeat the phrase until you consistently play it correctly.
5. Start from the beginning of the tune, and play through the next phrase. Apply the same learning steps to this phrase as you did to the first. When you can play the first and second phrases together without error, begin working on the third phrase, and then the fourth, until you can play them all without error. Then work on playing the tune up to speed while concentrating on good position, tone, and intonation.

4. Jam with other musicians. After you have memorized your tunes and can play them at the speed of the recording, you are ready to jam. This is your reward for all of your hard work. Join a local fiddle, bluegrass or folk music society that sponsors regular jams. Go to music festivals and fiddle contests. Don't be shy about meeting people and asking them to jam or to show you a lick or two. Some of these meetings will turn into lasting friendships and regular jam opportunities.

The Parts of a Fiddle

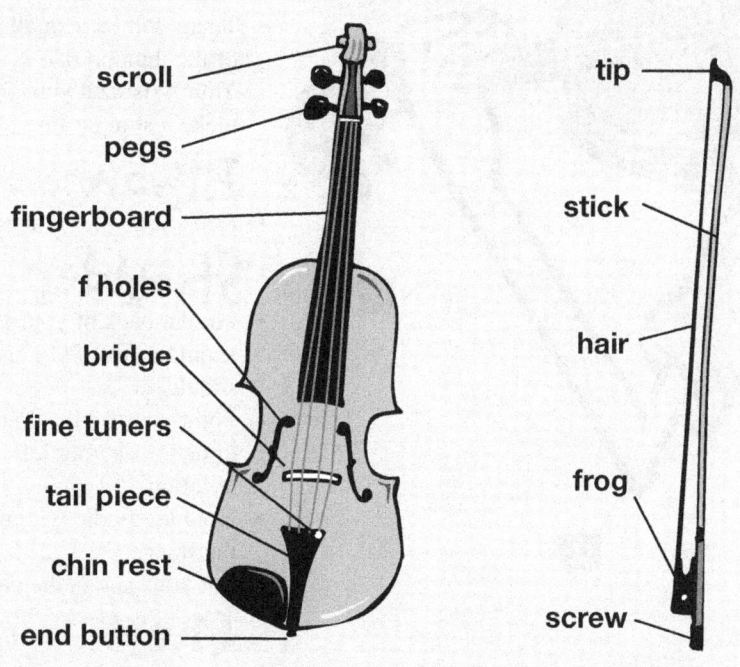

7

Bow and Fiddle Position

You will see fiddlers hold their instruments in all kinds of ways. Some hold the bow in the middle of the stick, some place the fiddle low on their chest and some play slouched with their legs crossed. Many of these players manage to play with decent tone and intonation. However, they tend to have a much more difficult time doing some of the more complicated fiddle and violin skills such as using upper positions and vibrato. Classical technique has evolved over hundreds of years to allow us to play the violin with the greatest ease and efficiency. If you want to be able to play any kind of music, no matter how difficult, learn the positions shown below. If you are very picky about your technique early on, and make sure your muscles memorize it correctly, you will have good position every time you pick up your fiddle without having to think about it.

Seven-Point Position Checklist

Memorize the following points in order and go through them before playing.

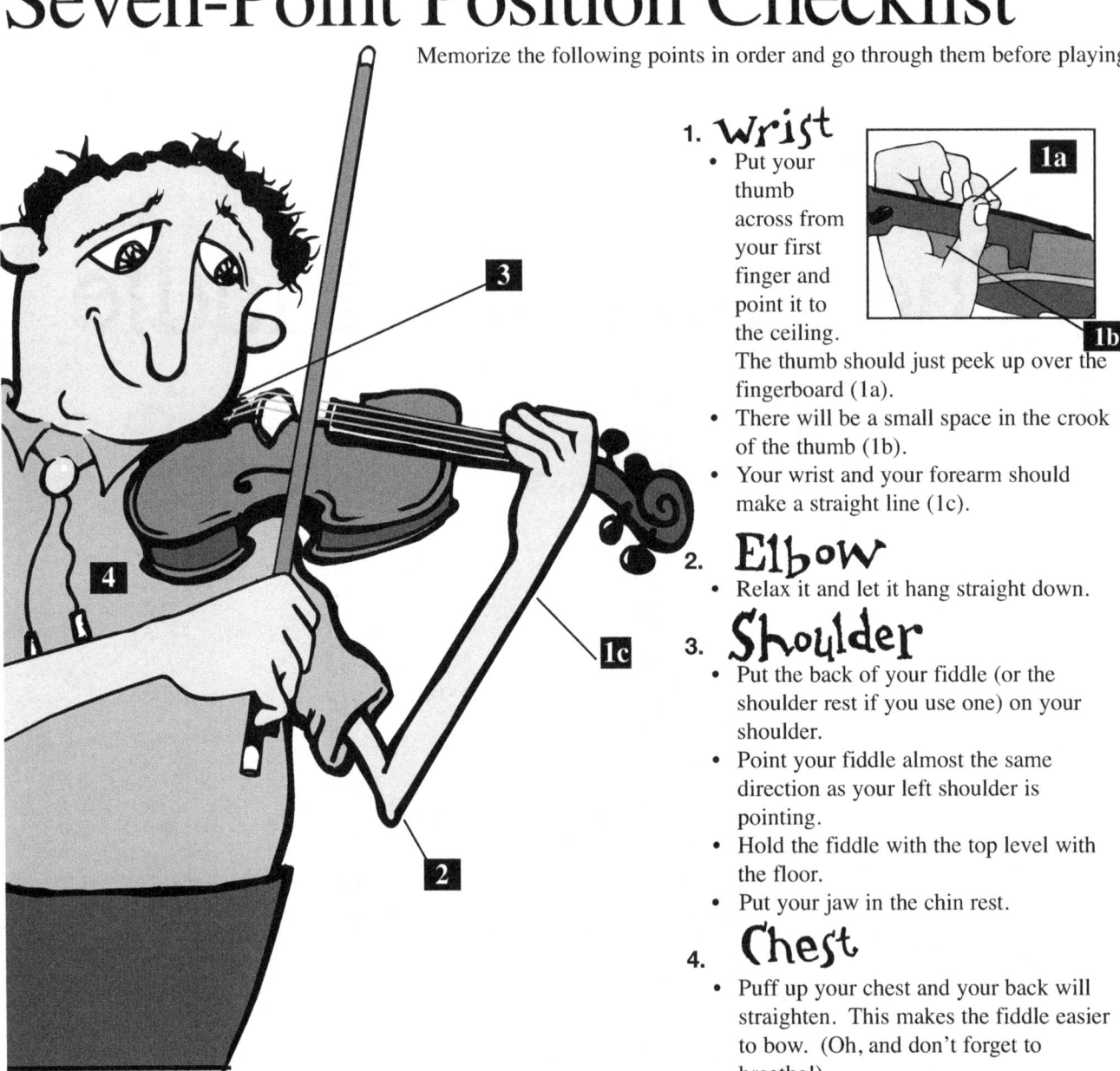

1. Wrist
- Put your thumb across from your first finger and point it to the ceiling. The thumb should just peek up over the fingerboard (1a).
- There will be a small space in the crook of the thumb (1b).
- Your wrist and your forearm should make a straight line (1c).

2. Elbow
- Relax it and let it hang straight down.

3. Shoulder
- Put the back of your fiddle (or the shoulder rest if you use one) on your shoulder.
- Point your fiddle almost the same direction as your left shoulder is pointing.
- Hold the fiddle with the top level with the floor.
- Put your jaw in the chin rest.

4. Chest
- Puff up your chest and your back will straighten. This makes the fiddle easier to bow. (Oh, and don't forget to breathe!)

5. Bow Hold Position

- You may hold the bow with your thumb either on the silver ring under the frog (5a), or in the cut-away notch of the frog (5b). There are skilled players who hold it either way.
- Your thumb should be slightly bent if under the frog and more bent if in the notch of the frog.
- The spot between the joints of your index finger should lie across the top of the bow (5c).
- Your middle and ring fingers should drape over the top of the bow (5d).
- The tip of your pinky finger should be above the end of the frog, and just ahead of the screw (5e).
- If the preceding points are done properly, your fingers will slant toward the tip of the bow.

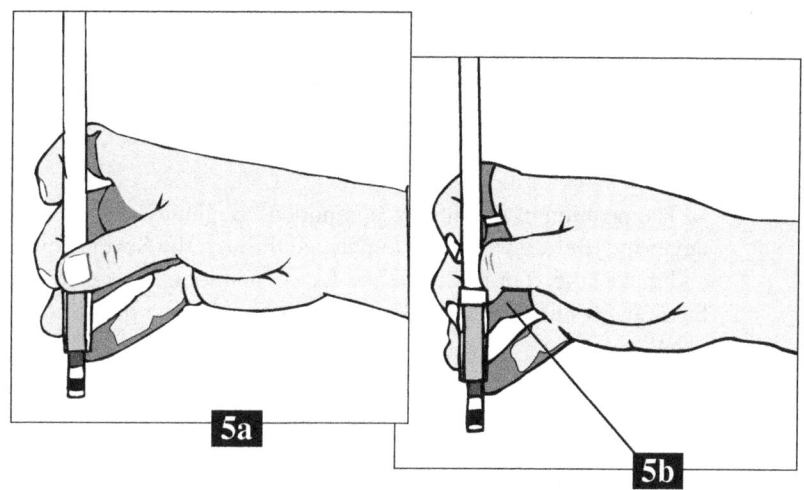

6. Bow on the "Highway"

- Bowing midway between the bridge and the end of the fingerboard will make your tone loud and rich.

7. Eyes

- Watch your fingering and bowing and you will be more aware of what you're doing.

Fingering Position

The position of the fingers is important to allow you to play the notes in tune and with the greatest dexterity. Before you begin to play, go through the Seven-Point Position Checklist beginning on page 8 and make sure your position is perfect. Then look in a mirror to compare your fingering position with the drawings below. Make sure you don't make one of the common mistakes at the bottom of this page!

Good Fingering Position

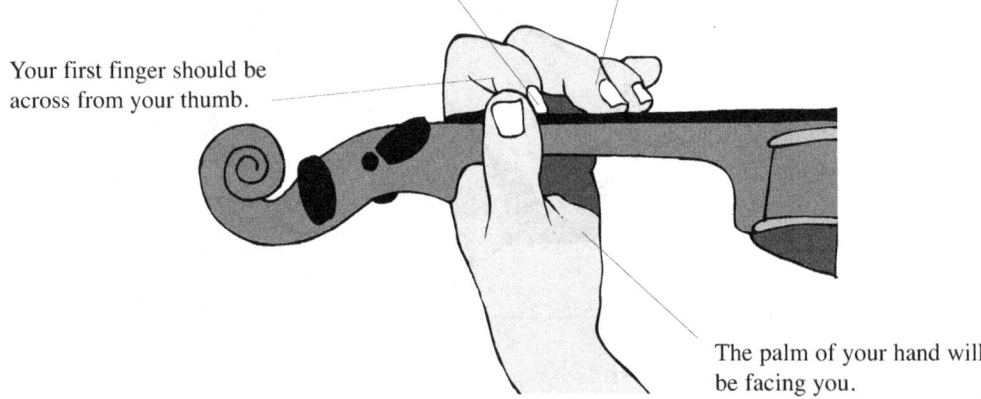

Imagine that the nail of your first finger is a mirror. Angle it so that you could see the reflection of your face in it.

The second and third fingers are slanted more than the first finger is. When fingering the C♯ and D on the A string in tune, the two fingers are squished together.

Your first finger should be across from your thumb.

The palm of your hand will be facing you.

The Twisted Wrist Mistake / The Bent Wrist Mistake

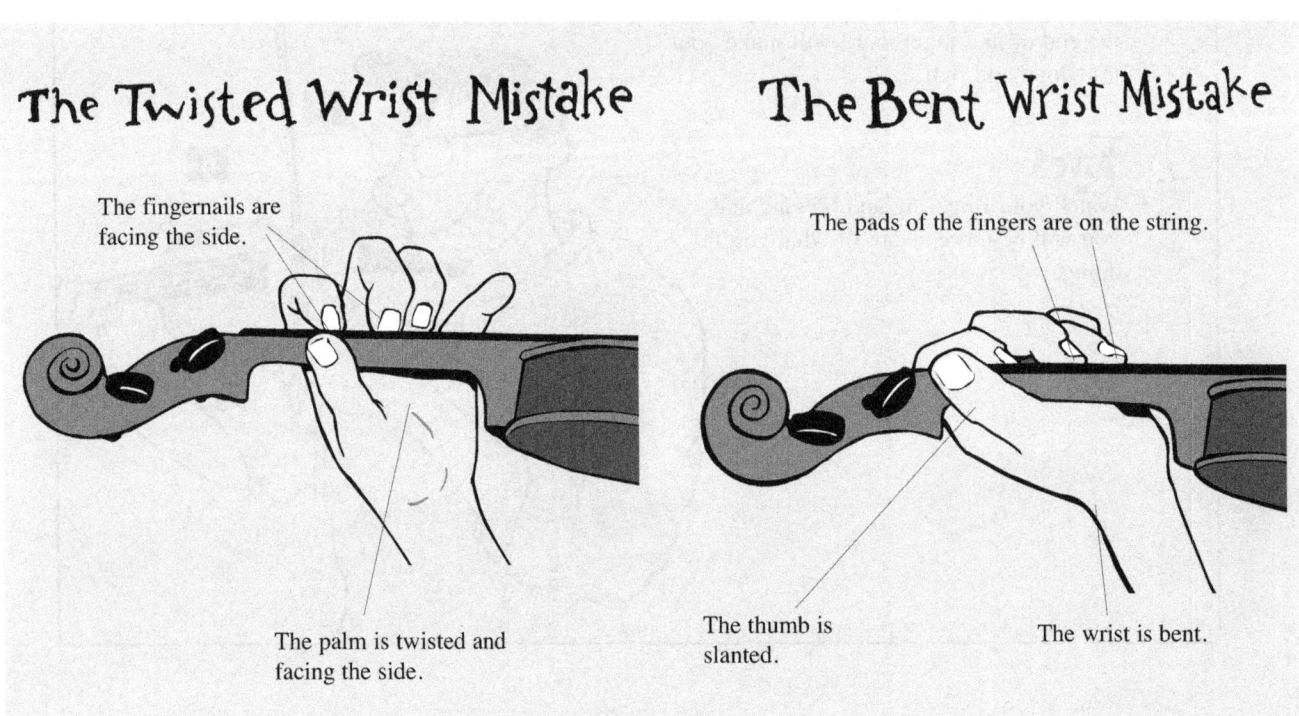

The fingernails are facing the side.

The palm is twisted and facing the side.

The pads of the fingers are on the string.

The thumb is slanted.

The wrist is bent.

Fingering Exercises

Consistently playing in tune is one of the most difficult skills in playing the fiddle. In order to have good intonation, you must both hear the note in your head and remember what it feels like to finger it correctly *before* you play it. This skill takes a great deal of careful practice.

Play the following scales. Play them very slowly and make sure you really *hear* each of the notes. Concentrate on each note being in tune and don't continue the scale if you hear a clunker; stop, and start over until you can play the scale perfectly in tune. Beginners should have their fingerboards marked with tape or dots by a teacher or skilled player to help with finger placement.

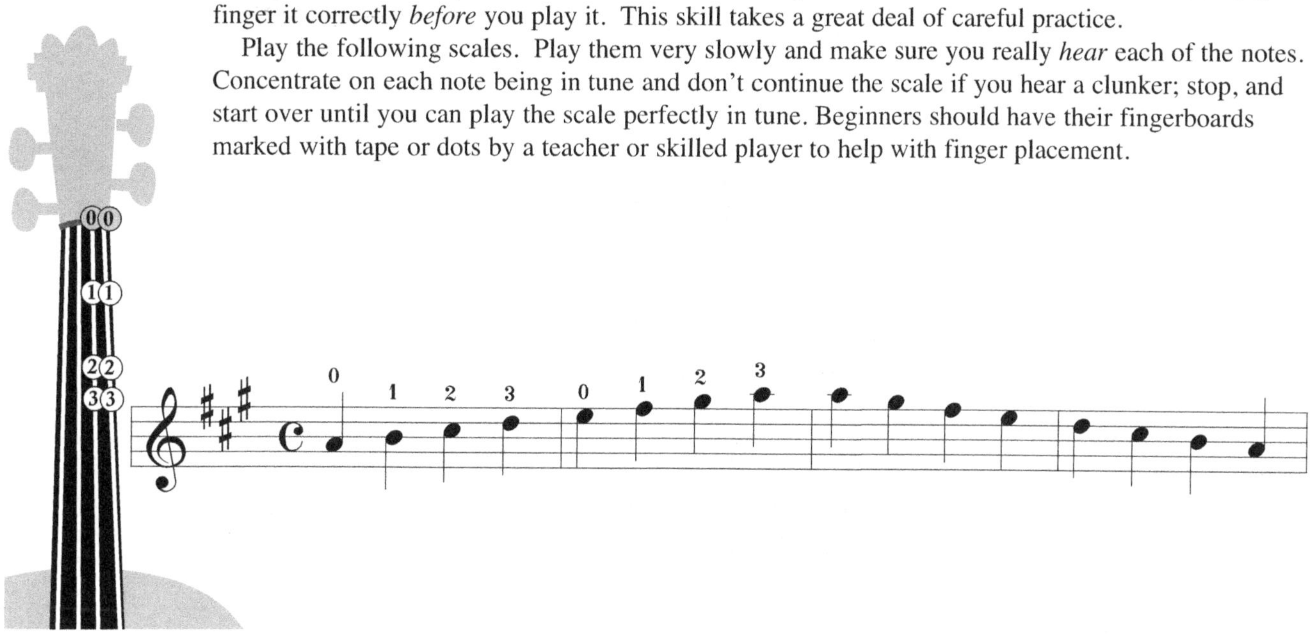

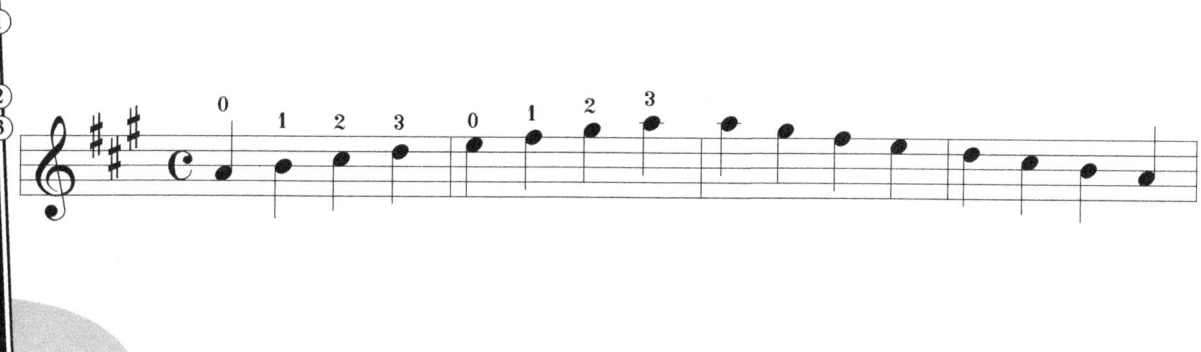

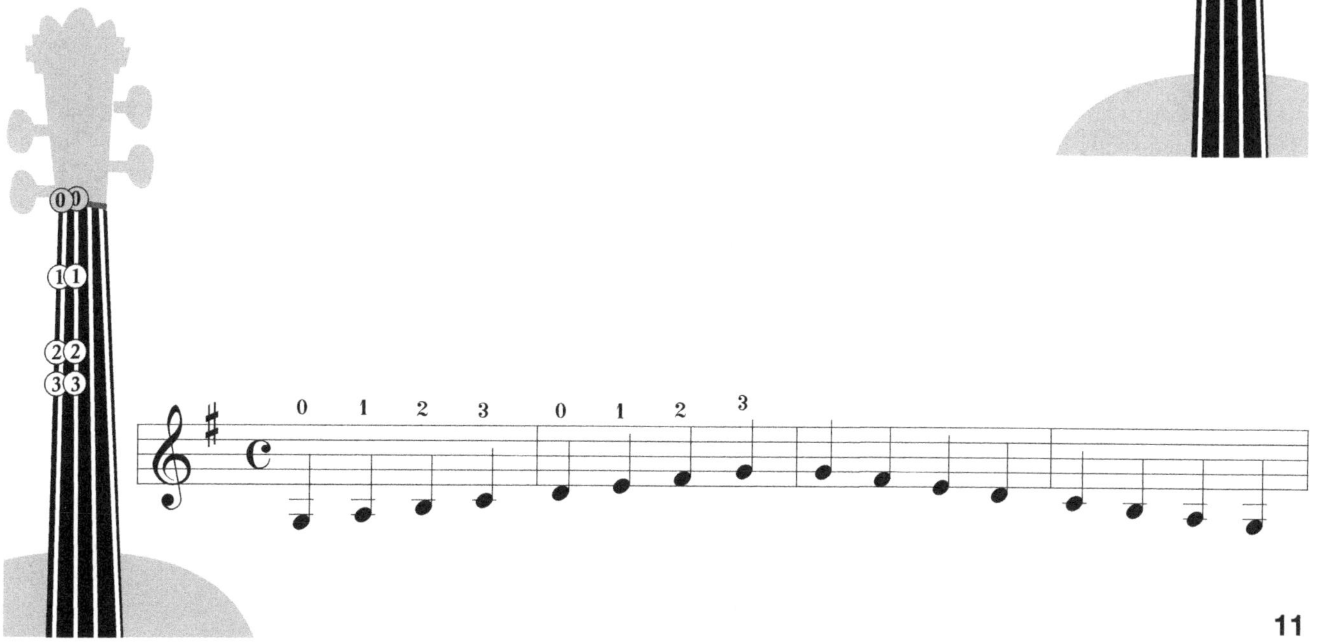

The Anatomy of a Fiddle Tune

A and B Parts

Most fiddle tunes have two parts to the melody, an A part and a B part, although tunes may have many more than two. The parts are usually four or eight measures long. Tunes that have this number of measures are called "square." Tunes that have more or fewer than four or eight measures per part are called "crooked." Because fiddle music was originally dance music (and continues to be used as dance music) a standard arrangement was necessary to coordinate the dancing and the music. If a "square" hoedown is played AABB (A part twice, B part twice), the beats will work out perfectly for most folk dances. The 32-bar form is the most common form in fiddle music.

Some tunes, however, are not played AABB. Of the tunes in this book, *Cindy* and *Buffalo Gals* have verses that are played and sung AB. *Arran Boat Song* is played AAB because the A part is half as long as the B part. *Crawdad Song* and *Stinky's Blues* are written in a style based on the blues, which is a different form altogether. Always practice tunes in their proper form.

Potato Introductions

When in a jam session, fiddlers often use a shuffle pattern called "potatoes" to get everyone starting together. Often called the "single shuffle" or the "Georgia shuffle," potatoes are four beats long and sound like "one 'tater, two 'tater, three 'tater, four."

Potatoes are only used for fast tunes such as hoedowns and reels in duple time (2/4 or 4/4). The double-stop you select for your potatoes should match the key of the tune and should be near in pitch to the first few notes of the melody.

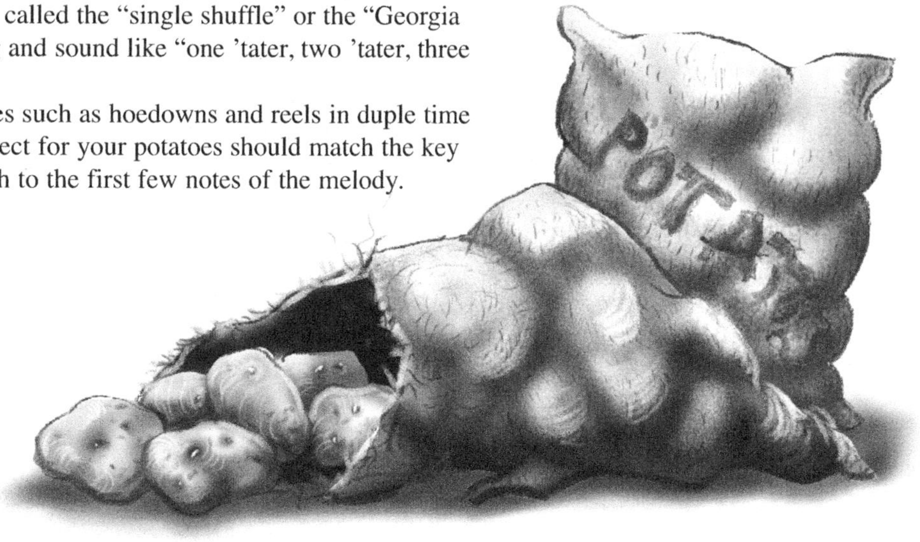

Potato Examples

Example 1 works for tunes in the key of A, such as *Boil 'em Cabbage Down*, *Shortnin' Bread*, and *Cripple Creek*.

Example 2 is for tunes in the key of D such as *Angelina Baker* and *Crawdad Song*.

Example 3 is another way you can kick off a tune in the key of D.

Example 4 is in the key of D and shows the pick-up notes for *Soldier's Joy*.

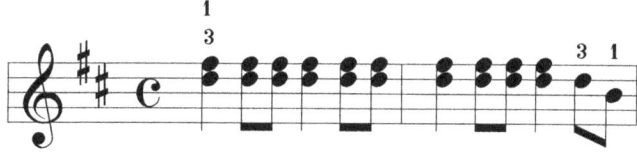

Example 5 is in the key of G and shows the pick-ups to *Turkey in the Straw*.

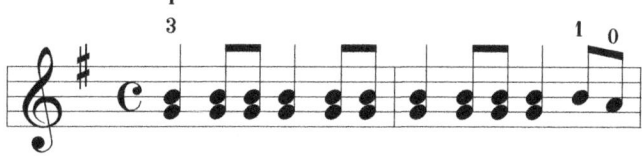

Endings

Just as the potatoes signal the other musicians in a jam when to start a tune, an ending tells them when to quit. The following are examples of some easy "shave and a haircut, two bits" endings. These may only be used on fast tunes in duple (2/4 or 4/4) time. More difficult endings are presented in *American Fiddle Method Volume 2*.

Example 1 is in the key of A and would work for tunes such as *Boil 'em Cabbage Down* and *Cripple Creek*.

Example 2 works for tunes in the key of D, such as *Soldier's Joy* and *Angelina Baker*.

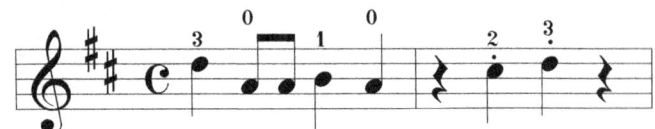

Example 3 could be played for *Red Wing*, and *Turkey in the Straw*, and any other hoedowns in the key of G.

Example 4 is also in the key of G but is an octave higher.

1 Boil 'em Cabbage Down

*This tune was first performed in minstrel shows before the American Civil War.
"Hoe cake" is bread that slaves baked on garden hoes over an open fire.*

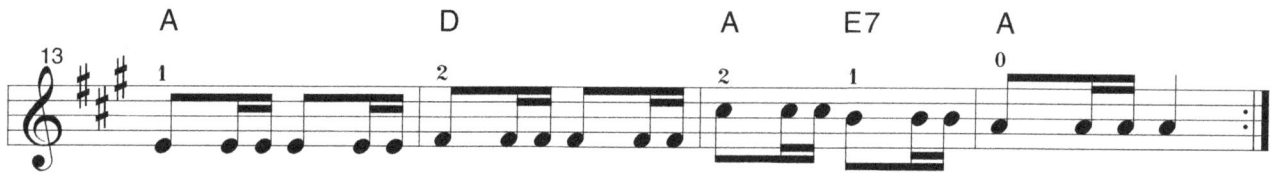

(*verses and chorus sung to A part*)

1. Went up on the mountain to give my horn a blow
   Thought I heard my true love say, "Yonder stands my beau"
   Raccoon and a 'possum running side by side
   Raccoon asked the 'possum, "Won't you be my bride?"

   •*chorus*•
   Boil 'em cabbage down boys, turn, turn the hoe cake brown
   The only song that I can sing is boil 'em cabbage down

2. Raccoon up a 'simmon tree, 'possum on the ground
   Raccoon said to the 'possum, "Shake them 'simmons down"
   Jay bird died with the whooping cough, sparrow died with the colic
   Along came a frog with a fiddle on his back,
      inquiring his way to the frolic

3. Took my dog to the blacksmith's shop to have his mouth made small
   He turned around a time or two, and swallowed the shop and all

15

Shortnin' Bread

This is a traditional African-American song.

(verses sung to A part, chorus sung to B)

1. Three little children lyin' in a bed
   Two was sick and one nearly dead
   Sent for the doctor, the doctor said
   "Feed those children on shortnin' bread"

   •*chorus*•
   Momma's little baby loves shortnin', shortnin'
   Momma's little baby loves shortnin' bread
   Momma's little baby loves shortnin', shortnin'
   Momma's little baby loves shortnin' bread

2. Put on the skillet, put on the lid
   Momma gonna bake a little shortnin' bread
   That ain't all she's gonna do
   Momma gonna make a little coffee, too

3. I slip to the kitchen, lift up the lid
   Filled my pocket full of shortnin' bread
   Stole the skillet, stole the lid
   Stole the gal makin' shortnin' bread

4. Caught me with the skillet, they caught me with the lid
   They caught me with the gal makin' shortnin' bread
   Six dollars for the skillet, six dollars for the lid
   And six months in jail eatin' shortnin' bread

3 Cripple Creek

This American folk song comes from the Appalachian Mountains.

(verse sung to A part, chorus sung to B)
Goin' up Cripple Creek, goin' on the run
Goin' up Cripple Creek to have some fun
Pull my britches to my knees
Wade old Cripple Creek as I please

•chorus•
Goin' up Cripple Creek goin' on the run
Goin' up Cripple Creek to have some fun
Goin' up Cripple Creek in a whirl
Goin' up Cripple Creek to see my girl

4 Camptown Races

Stephen Foster wrote this song about horse racing in 1850.

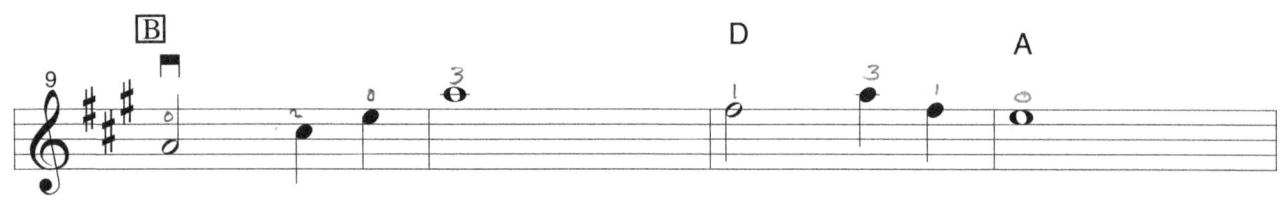
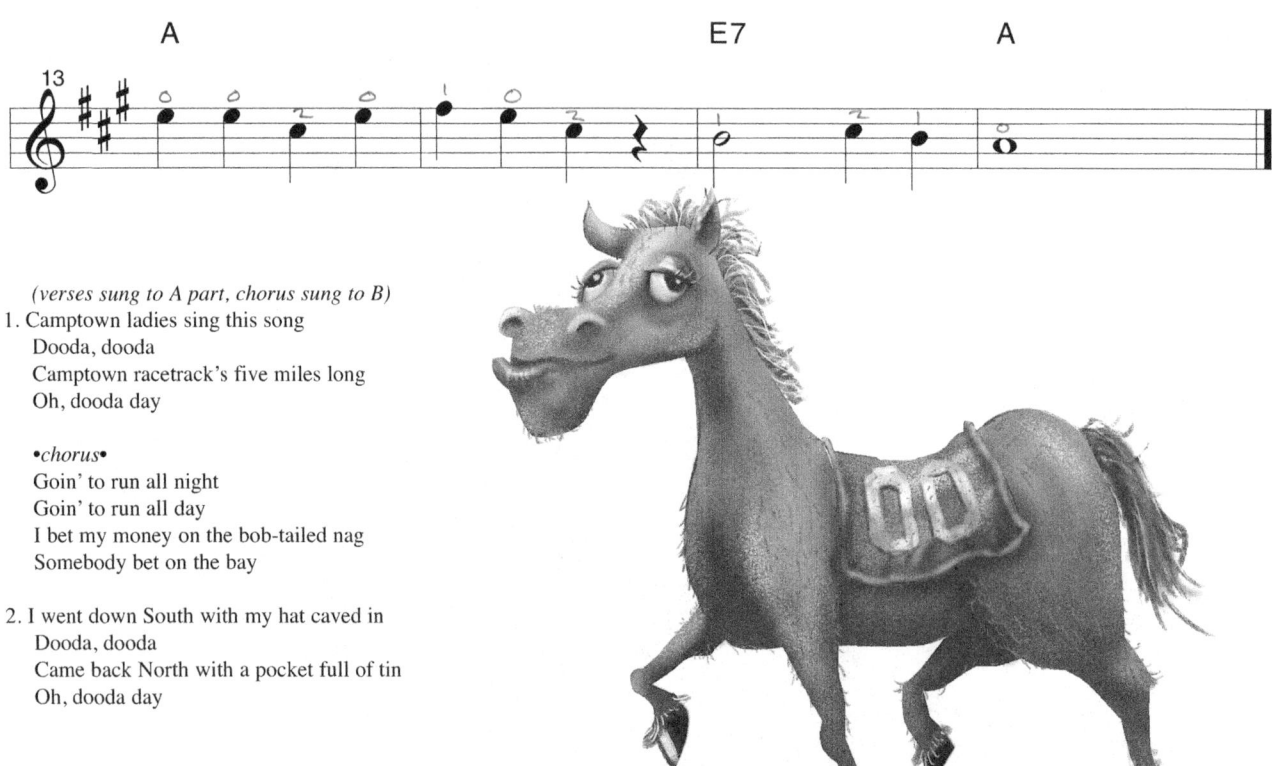

(verses sung to A part, chorus sung to B)

1. Camptown ladies sing this song
   Dooda, dooda
   Camptown racetrack's five miles long
   Oh, dooda day

   •chorus•
   Goin' to run all night
   Goin' to run all day
   I bet my money on the bob-tailed nag
   Somebody bet on the bay

2. I went down South with my hat caved in
   Dooda, dooda
   Came back North with a pocket full of tin
   Oh, dooda day

5 Angelina Baker

This American folk song was written before the Civil War.

(verses and chorus sung to B part)

1. Angelina Baker she lives on the village green
   The way that I love her beats all to be seen
   Angelina Baker her age is forty-three
   I gave her candy by the peck but she won't marry me

   •*chorus*•
   Angelina Baker, Angelina Baker
   Angelina Baker, Angelina Baker

2. Angeline is handsome and Angeline is tall
   She broke her little ankle from dancing in the hall
   She won't do the bacon because she is too stout
   She makes cookies by the peck and throws the coffee out

3. Last time I saw her was at the county fair
   Her man he chased me half-way home and told me to stay there
   She taught me to weep and she taught me to moan
   Angeline she taught me to weep and beat on the old jawbone

6 Buffalo Gals

A minstrel singer named Cool White wrote this song in 1844 about the beautiful gals of Buffalo, New York.

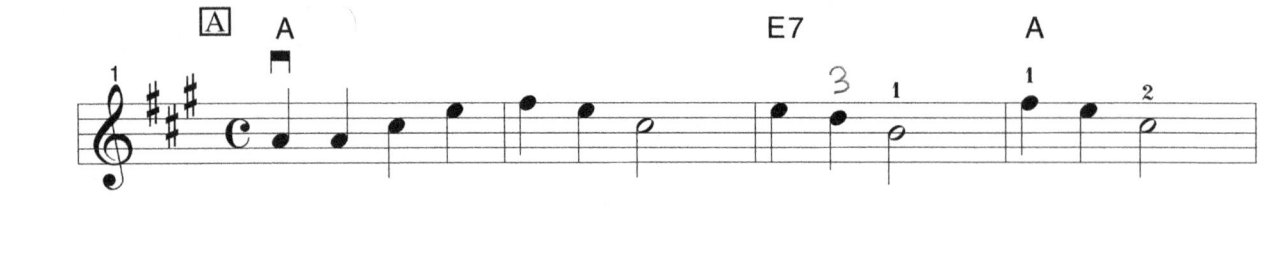

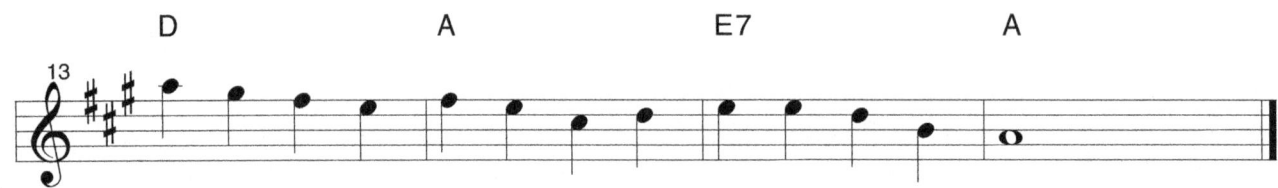

(verses sung to A part, chorus sung to B)

1. As I was walking down the street
   Down the street, down the street
   A pretty girl I chanced to meet
   And we danced by the light of the moon

   •*chorus*•
   Buffalo gals won't you come out tonight
   Come out tonight, come out tonight
   Buffalo gals won't you come out tonight
   And dance by the light of the moon

2. I asked her if she'd stop and talk
   Stop and talk, stop and talk
   Her feet covered up the whole sidewalk
   She was fair to view

3. I asked her if she'd be my wife
   Be my wife, be my wife
   Then I'd be happy all my life
   If she'd marry me

4. I danced with a gal with a hole in her stocking
   And her heel kept a-rockin' and her knees kept a-knockin'
   I danced with a gal with a hole in her stocking
   And we danced by the light of the moon

The Fourth Finger

As you begin learning to play the fourth finger, make sure your position is good. Don't allow your thumb and your first finger to slide up. Just let your fourth finger reach into position. Match the fourth finger on the A string with the open E string (they are both E notes).

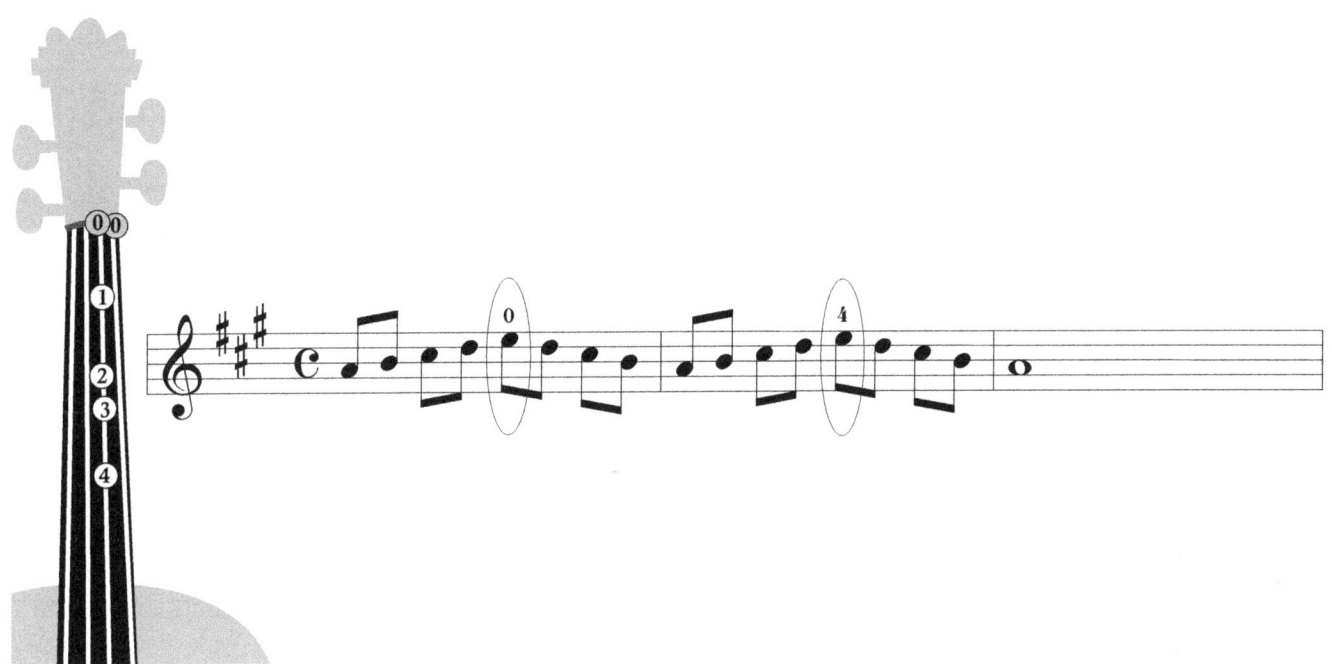

Use the same technique now on the E string as you did on the A string.

7 Cindy

This is an antebellum, Southern American folk song.

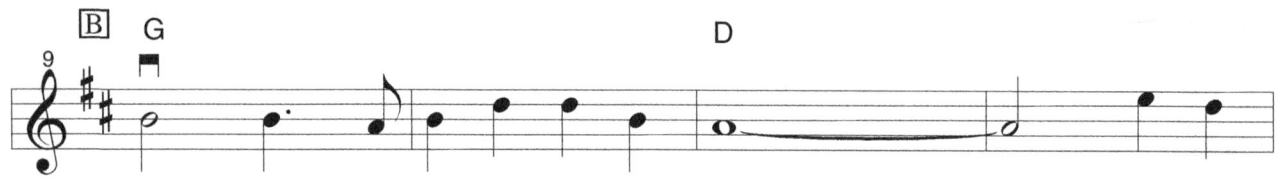

(verses sung to the A part, chorus sung to B)

1. You ought to see my Cindy
   She lives way down South
   She's so sweet the honey bees
   Swarm around her mouth

   •*chorus*•
   Get along home, Cindy, Cindy
   Get along home
   Get along home, Cindy, Cindy
   I'll marry you someday

2. When first I seen my Cindy
   She was standing by the door
   Shoes and stockings in her hand
   And her little bare feet on the floor

3. Wish I was an apple
   Hangin' on a tree
   Every time my Cindy'd pass
   She'd take a bite of me

4. Cindy in the springtime
   Cindy in the fall
   If I can't have my Cindy, gal
   I'll have no gal at all

How's Your Wrist Position?

8 Crawdad Song

This African-American song is about crayfish.

1. You get a line and I'll get a pole, honey
   You get a line and I'll get a pole, babe
   You get a line and I'll get a pole
   We'll go fishin' in that crawdad hole
   Honey, sugar baby, mine

2. Yonder comes a man with a sack on his back, honey
   Yonder . . . back, babe
   Yonder . . . back
   Packing all the crawdads he can pack
   Honey, sugar baby, mine

3. The man fell down and he bust his sack, honey
   The man . . . sack, babe
   The man . . . sack
   Look at them crawdads crawling back
   Honey, sugar baby, mine

4. What you gonna do when the lake runs dry. . .
   Sit on the bank and watch the crawdads die. . .

5. What you gonna do when the crawdads die, honey. . .
   Sit on the bank until I cry. . .

6. Look at that crawdad crawlin' round, honey. . .
   He's the mayor of that crawdad town. . .

7. I heard the duck say to the drake, honey. . .
   "There ain't no crawdads in this lake. . ."

The Low Second Finger

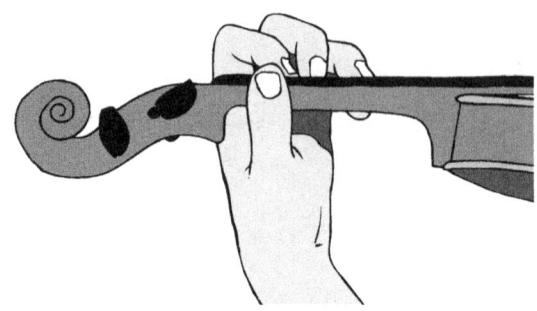

Some tunes are in keys that require you to play a low second finger. When both the first and the second fingers are down and in tune, the second finger should almost touch your first. Be careful not to flat your first finger.

Play the following exercise with your second finger in the regular high position.

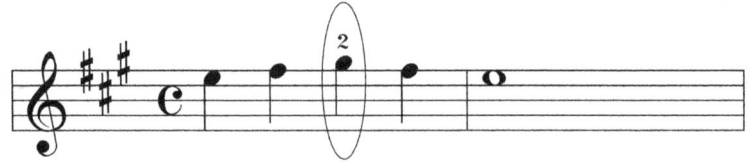

Now play the exercise with your second finger in the low position. It will almost touch your first finger.

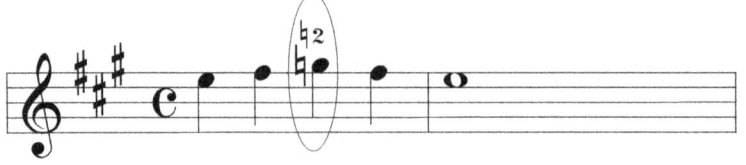

Now add the third finger to the exercise. Realize that the first and third finger positions on the E string have not changed. The new placement of the second finger, however, will make your third finger feel stretched when it is in tune. Listen carefully to your fingering, and be very picky about playing in tune. Repeat this exercise many times.

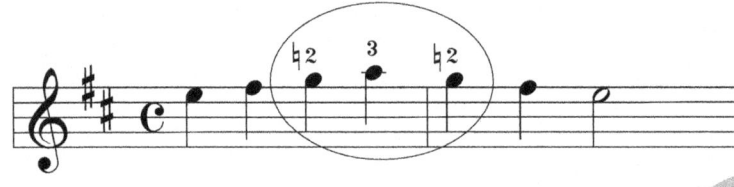

24

Now practice the same fingering on the A string. Here is the high second finger.

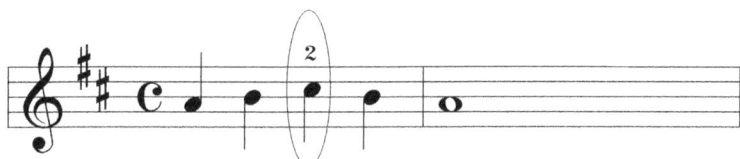

Now play the low second finger. Remember, it should almost touch your first finger.

You can now add the third finger. Don't let your second finger become sharp when you add the third.

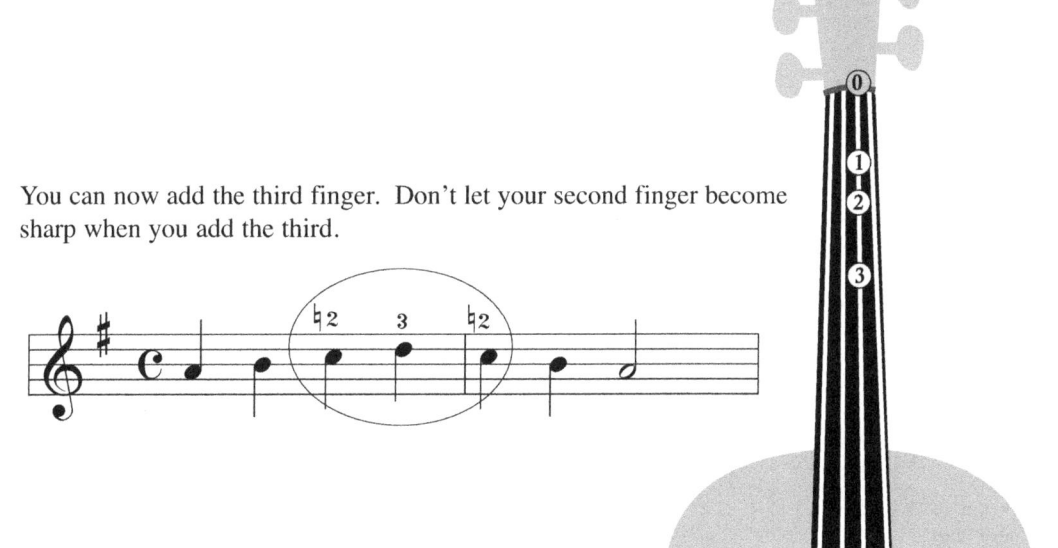

9 Old Joe Clark

This tune was written before 1840 and is thought to be about an African-American man from Kentucky.

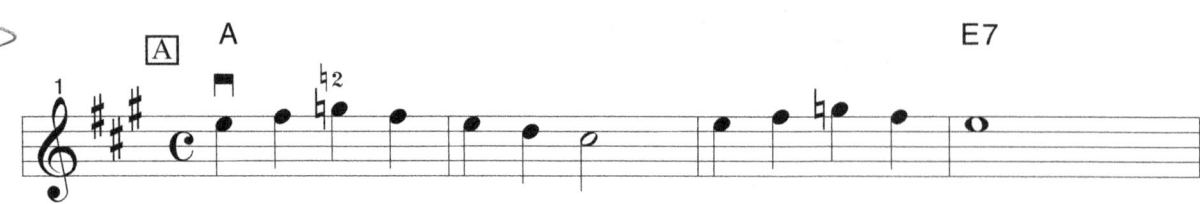

(verses sung to A part, chorus sung to B)

1. I used to live on the mountain top
   Now I live in town
   I'm staying at the big hotel
   A-courting Betsy Brown

2. Old Joe Clark, he had a house
   Sixteen stories high
   And every story in that house
   Was filled with chicken pie

   •*chorus*•
   Fare thee well, Old Joe Clark
   Fare thee well, I say
   Fare thee well, Old Joe Clark
   I'm a-going away

3. Old Joe had a chicken coop
   Sixteen stories high
   And every chicken in that coop
   Turned into chicken pie

4. Old Joe Clark, he had a mule
   His name was Morgan Brown
   And every tooth in that mule's head
   Was sixteen inches 'round

5. I went down to Old Joe's house
   He invited me to supper
   I stubbed my toe on the table leg
   And stuck my nose in the butter

6. Old Joe Clark's a mean old man
   I'll tell you the reason why
   He blew his nose in my corn bread
   And called it pumpkin pie

26

write note names **10 Soldier's Joy**

*This fiddle tune comes from the British Isles and is played throughout the world.
Soldiers called their pay day "soldier's joy."*

Arran Boat Song

This type of slow, mournful Irish tune is called an "air." This tune is named after islands off the coast of Ireland.

Down-Driven Bowing and Corrective Slurs

One of the many aspects of fiddle music that makes it so fun to play is the almost endless variations of bowing. There are as many ways to bow a tune as there are fiddlers. However, before you are set free to explore your own bowing, you should master what I call "Down-Driven Bowing."

Gravity naturally gives your down-bows a slight accent and makes up-bows slightly weaker. When playing passages of a series of eighth or sixteenth notes as "saw strokes" (one bow stroke per note), the rhythm sounds best when down-bows are on the beat notes. This is Down-Driven Bowing and it gives tunes good rhythmic drive.

Keep in mind that Down-Driven Bowing is not an end-all bow pattern. Master fiddlers mix a large number of patterns of slurs and saw strokes and often deliberately play phrases with up-driven bow strokes to create syncopation. However, I have found that students who master Down-Driven Bowing have a great foundation from which to explore a world of creative bowing. Volume 2 covers other patterns and how to make up your own bowing. A down-bow is written as a staple, ⊓ , and an up-bow is a ∨ .

This section will teach you to use slurs to "correct" the bow's direction. It takes time to internalize the feeling of this skill and a lot of practice before it becomes automatic. Therefore, before exploring your own interpretation of bowing, memorize the bowing for each tune as written in this book. Teaching yourself to tap your foot on the beat while you play helps you to feel where to put in a corrective slur. If you are adding them correctly, you will notice that your down bows are going with your foot tap nearly all the time.

In fig.1, the slight accent of your down-bows landing on the beat notes make a rhythm like "Da, da, Da, da, Da, da, Da, da." This has a good rhythmic drive. However, in fig. 2, the bowing is reversed and up-bows are landing on the beat making a jerky-sounding rhythm like "da, Da, da, Da, da, Da, da Da."

Down-Driven Bowing: Notice that all of the down-bows fall on beat notes.

Reversed Bowing: Here up-bows fall on the beat. This will have a jerky-sounding rhythm.

29

Some fiddle tunes consist exclusively of eighth notes (such as *Devil's Dream* from AFM Volume 2). If we started one of these tunes on a down-bow, our down-bows would land on the beat notes through the entire tune. However, most tunes have more rhythmic variety than this. Quarter notes mixed in with eighth notes can reverse the bow direction relative to the beat (fig. 3). There are three ways to prevent playing the phrase with reversed bowing: adding "Corrective Slurs" (described below), resetting the bow (discussed on page 35), and adding extra notes (to be covered in future volumes).

Reversed Bowing: Without any slurs, the fourth beat of measure 1 and the first and second beats of measure 2 are up-bows and therefore reversed.

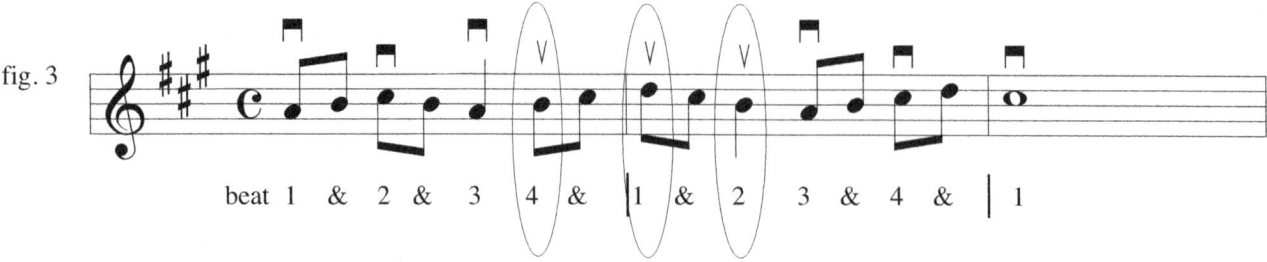

Down-Driven Bowing with Corrective Slurs After Quarter Note: Here the bow direction is corrected by slurring the two eighth notes that come **after** the quarter note, thereby allowing us to play the next beat note on a down-bow.

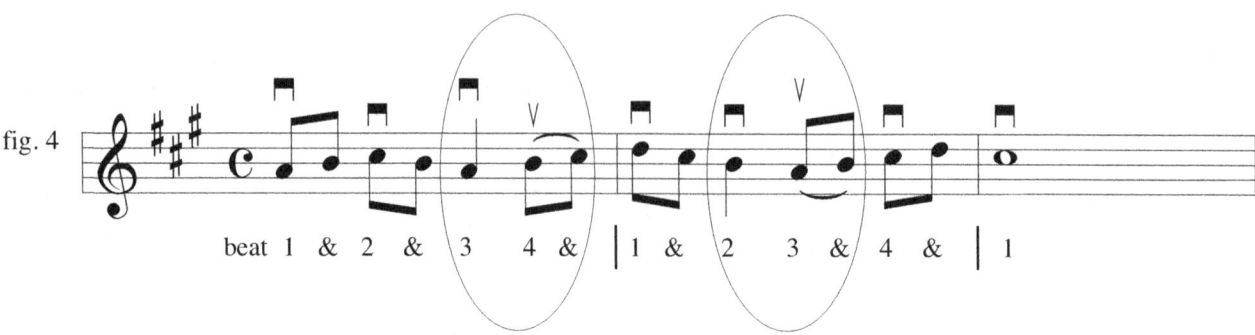

Down-Driven Bowing with Corrective Slurs Before Quarter Note: You may also slur the quarter note with the eighth note that comes **before** it. Both this example and the one above are common and are used in tunes in this book.

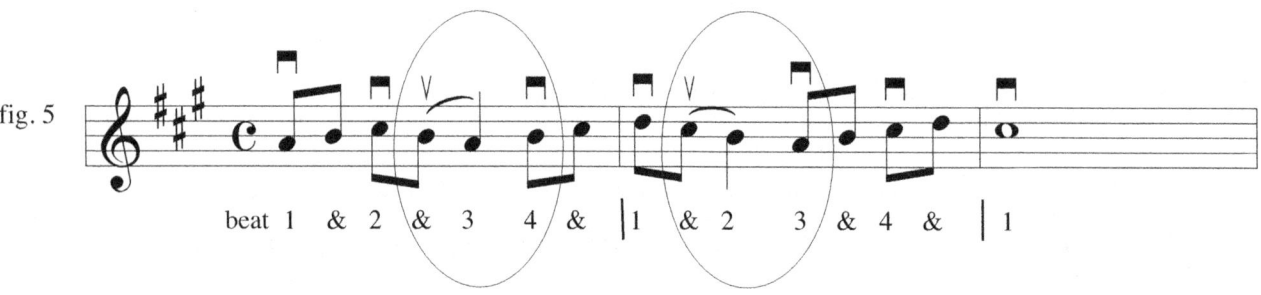

12 Bonaparte's Retreat

This tune comes from the Appalachian Mountains.

13 Country Waltz

This old-time American tune is played throughout the United States.

14 Red Haired Boy

This Irish tune is also known as "The Little Beggar Man."
The beginning of this tune shows a way to use a slur to maintain down-driven bowing. When you start the tune, play separate saw strokes. When you play the first ending, you will end down-bow, so add an up-bow slur on the first two notes of the tune as you repeat.

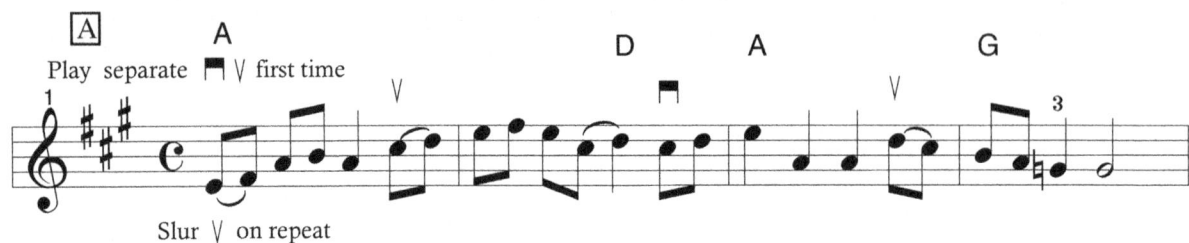

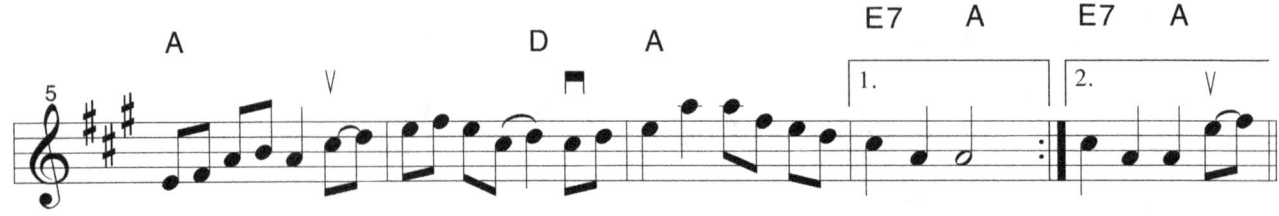

15 Girl I Left Behind Me

The melody can be traced to the 1750s in England and is still often played by the British Army. Although traditionally played with a straight-eighth rhythm, I recorded this one with a swing rhythm. It has a "long, short, long, short" feel to it. Feel free to experiment with swing rhythm on other fiddle tunes in this book. It is really fun to play.

Be a FiddlePal!
Books, Videos, Instruction, Fun
www.fiddlepal.com

16 Southwind

This tune is an Irish waltz.

Bow Reset

As mentioned in the section on slurs, you can correct the bow direction or add emphasis to a note by playing a bow reset. A bow reset is simply lifting the bow off the string after a down-bow, and replacing near the frog to play another down-bow. Make sure you set the bow near the frog rather than in the middle of the bow; otherwise, it will bounce. Practice the following exercise and reset at the commas.

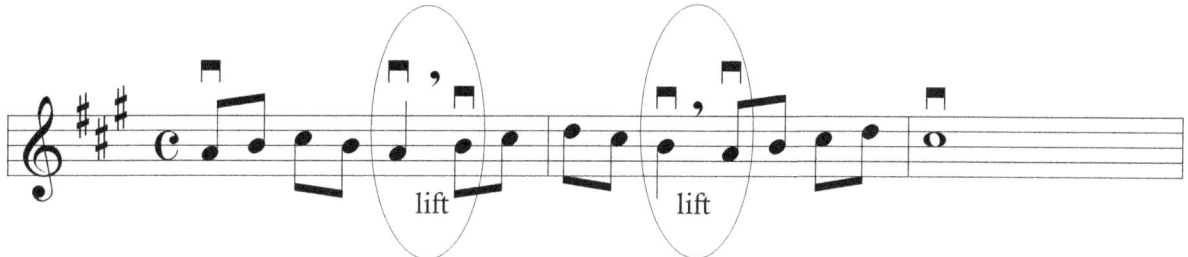

Staccato Slurs

A staccato slur is like a regular slur except the notes are separate sounding. Play the first note, stop the bow, and play the next note continuing in the same bow direction. You can do staccato slurs both up-bow and down-bow. Practice these exercises.

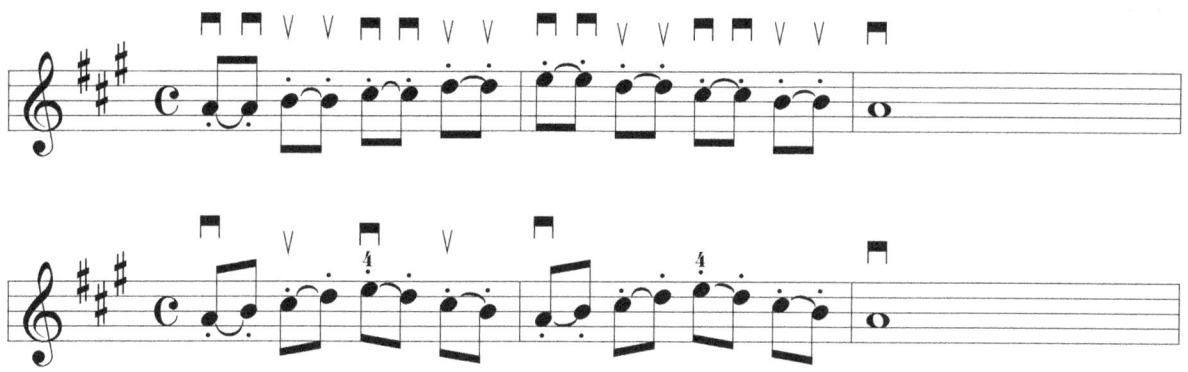

You will often see ⊓ ⊓ or V V in music without a comma or a slur. Remember that ⊓ ⊓ always means reset with a lift, and V V always means stop the bow with a staccato slur. The dotted slur will help you remember to stop the bow, then keep going to finish the up bow.

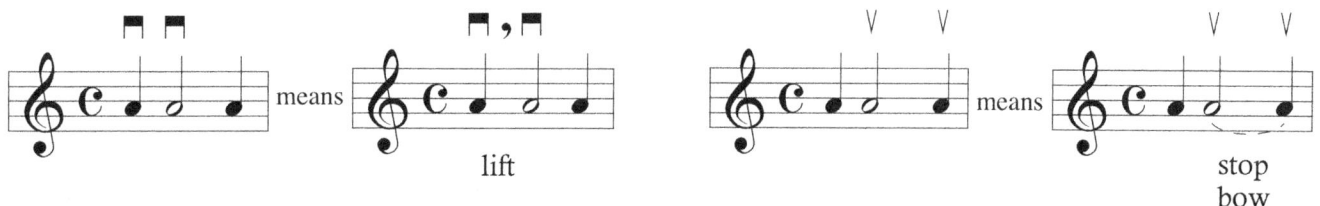

35

17 Red Wing

This song is about an American-Indian girl who is saddened by the loss of her sweetheart in battle. It was written by Thurland Cattaway and Kerry Mills in 1907.

Da Capo

18 Cairo

This tune is probably written about Cairo, Illinois (pronounced kay-roe), on the southern tip of Illinois near the borders of Kentucky and Missouri.

(verses sung to A part, chorus sung to B)

1. Goin' down to Cairo
   Goodbye, Magpie
   Goin' down to Cairo
   Goodbye, Liza Jane

   •chorus•
   Black them boots and make them shine
   Goodbye, Magpie
   Black them boots and make them shine
   Goodbye, Liza Jane

2. Oh how I love her
   And ain't that a shame
   Oh how I love her
   Goodbye, Liza Jane

3. I ain't got time to kiss you, now
   I'm sorry, I'm sorry
   I ain't got time to kiss you, now
   Goodbye, Liza Jane

19 Turkey in the Straw

*This is a Midwestern tune first played in the 1830s.
Over the years, endless verses have been written to its melody.*

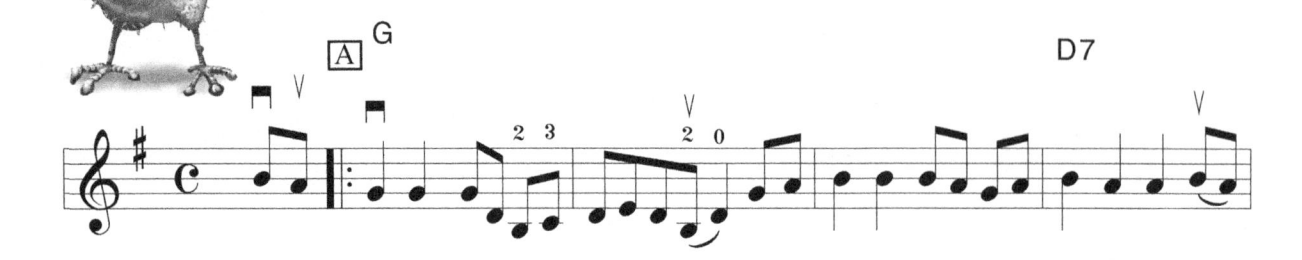

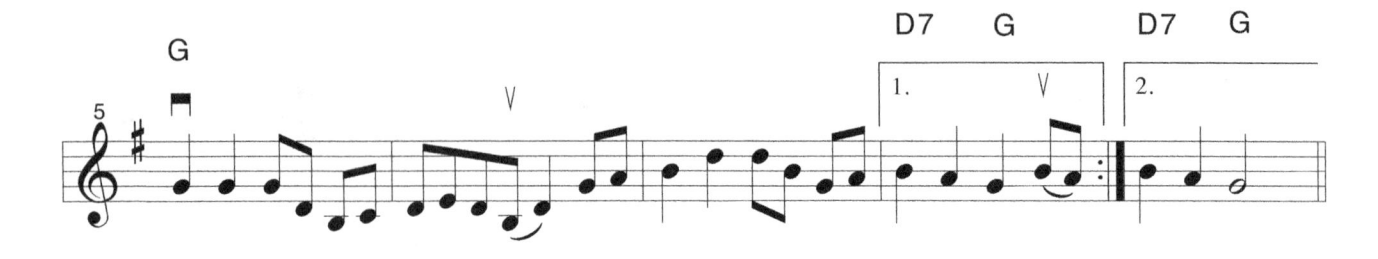

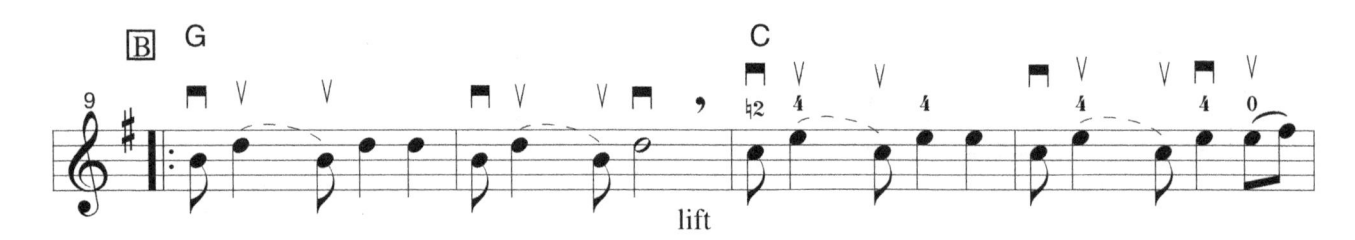

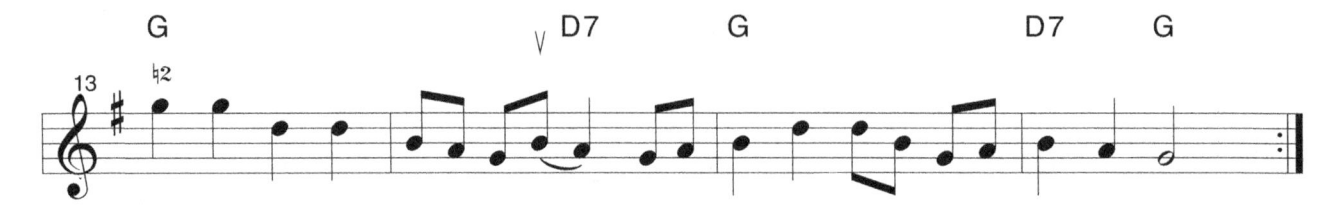

(verses sung to A part, chorus sung to B)

1. Oh, I had a little chicken and it wouldn't lay an egg
   So I poured hot water up and down its leg
   Oh, the little chicken cried and the little chicken begged
   And the little chicken laid me a hard boiled egg

   •*chorus*•
   Turkey in the straw (haw, haw, haw)
   Turkey in the hay (hey, hey, hey)
   Roll 'em up, pad 'em down, any way at all
   Play a little tune called Turkey in the Straw

2. Did you ever go fishing on a hot summer day
   And see the little fishies swimming up and down the way
   With their hands in their pockets and their pockets in their pants
   Did you ever see a fishy do a hootchy kootchy dance

3. I went to Toledo and I walked around the block
   And I ran right in to a bakery shop
   I took me a doughnut hot off the grease
   And I handed the lady a five-cent piece
   She looked at the nickel and she looked at me
   She said, "This nickel's no good to me"
   "There's a hole in the middle you can see right through"
   Says I, "There's a hole in the doughnut too"

The High Third Finger

You will need to use a high third finger for some tunes. The position of high third finger is between the regular third finger spot and the fourth finger spot. Make sure your first, second and fourth fingers do not change position. Play this exercise with the regular third finger.

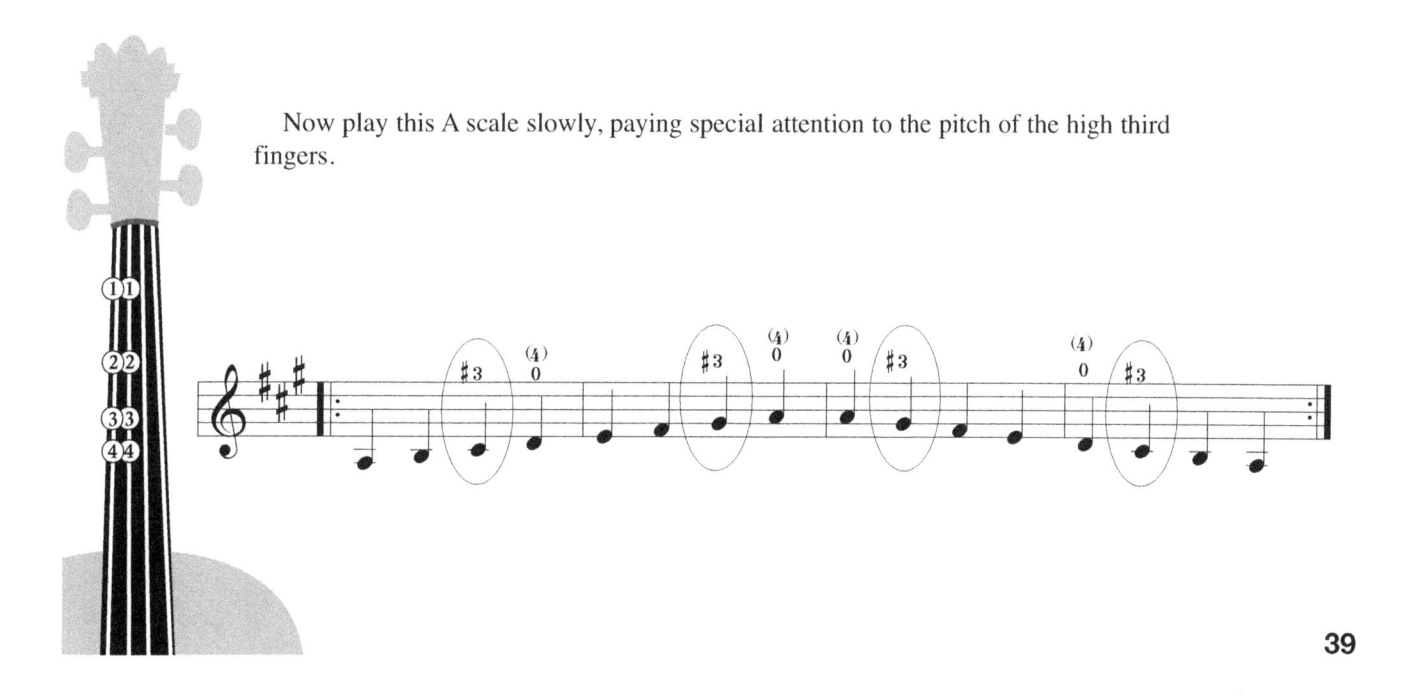

Now play this exercise with the high third finger.

Now play this A scale slowly, paying special attention to the pitch of the high third fingers.

39

20 Grandfather's Clock

Henry Clay Work wrote this song about a man and his special clock. Remember the V V means stop the bow on the string like a staccato slur, and ⊓ ⊓ means lift and reset the bow.

My grandfather's clock was too large for the shelf
So it stood ninety years on the floor
It was taller by half than the old man himself
'Though it weighed not a pennyweight more

It was bought on the morn of the day that he was born
And was always his treasure and pride
But it stopped short, never to go again
When the old man died

Ninety years without slumbering (tic, toc, tic, toc)
His life seconds numbering (tic, toc, tic, toc)
But it stopped short, never to go again
When the old man died

40

21 Wise Old Friend

© 1993 Brian Wicklund, BMI

I composed this waltz for the sound track for a film on a national park called the Boundary Waters Canoe Area. Ojibwa and French Canadians paddled their canoes through the chain of thousands of lakes between Canada and Minnesota carrying beaver pelts from Winnipeg to Lake Superior in the mid and late 1700s. The park is a very special place for me.

22 Stinky's Blues

© 1996 Brian Wicklund, BMI
This tune follows the 12-bar (measure) blues format. The variations of
this tune are common in many blues tunes.

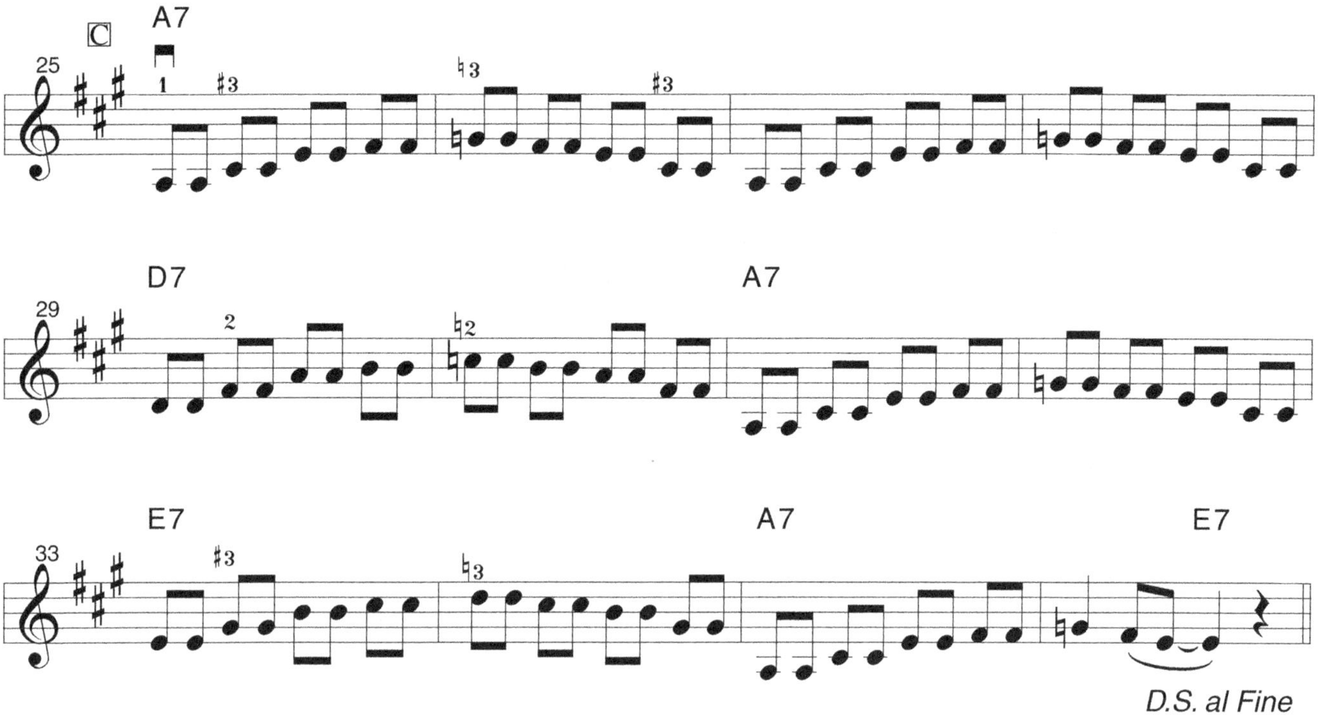
C
A7
25
D7
A7
29
E7
A7
E7
33
D.S. al Fine

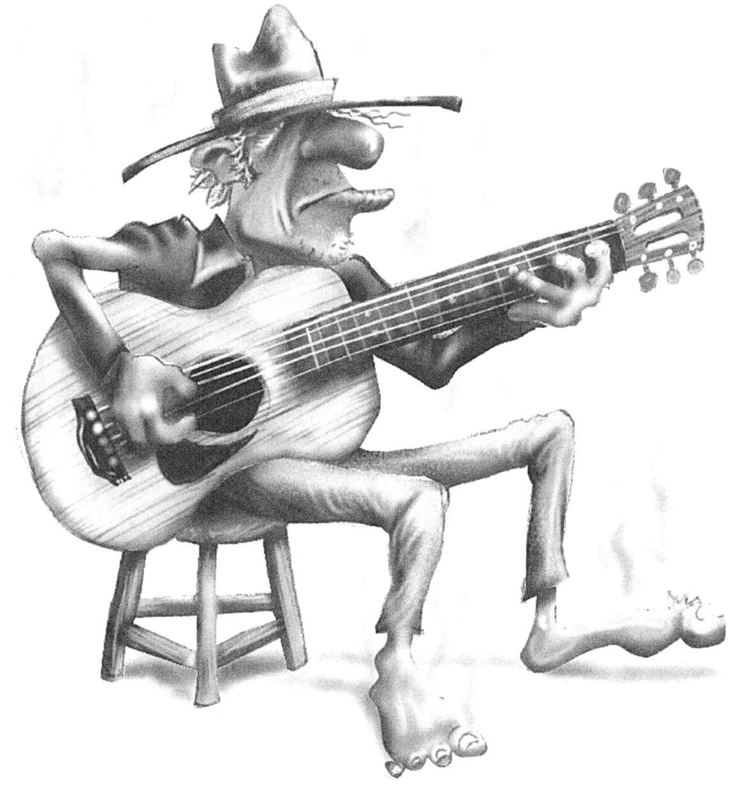

Creating Your Own Variations

One of the most enjoyable aspects of fiddle music is the room for individual creativity. Once you know the basic way to play a tune, you can make up your own variations. I have included two techniques in this book to get you started in that direction: drones and slides. More advanced skills will be covered in *American Fiddle Method Volume 2*.

You will notice that I do not include variations for all of the tunes in this book. I have chosen to write out only those that demonstrate some aspect of the techniques. This is to encourage you to come up with your own combinations of drones and slides. Once you can play the following variations, you will have the skills to apply to the rest of the tunes in the book.

For most of the tunes on the recording I first play the basic version, then the drone, then the slide, and finally I demonstrate how you can combine all of the variations. The exceptions are tunes where the variations do not really work well with the tune. Learn the following drone and slide examples, then apply them to other tunes in the book. Finally, combine the techniques and explore creating your own way to play the tune.

Drone and Double-Stop Variations

Fiddle players often add harmonies to the melody by playing two notes at once. A double-stop is any combination of two notes, whereas a drone is specifically a constant note played along with the melody, sounding like a bagpipe. Because most fiddle tunes are in the keys of A, D and G, fiddlers can often get a pleasing drone-type harmony by simply playing an adjacent, open string. The choice of which open string or fingered note to play depends upon which one harmonizes best with the chord.

You will find, however, that drones and double-stops do not work in every song. Delicate tunes and those with intricate fingering sound too heavy with drones. For those reasons, there are a number of tunes on the recording in which I don't use them, or I use them sparingly. The following variations are listed in order of difficulty.

Shortnin' Bread Drone Variation

These variations of Shortnin' Bread *and* Camptown Races *show how you can drone the same two strings throughout, giving the tune a bagpipe-like sound.*

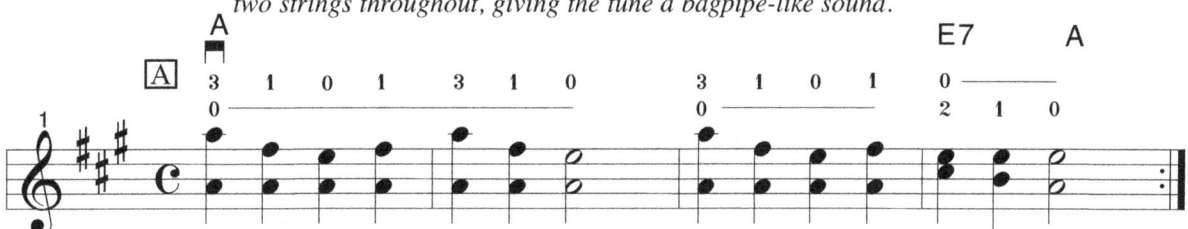

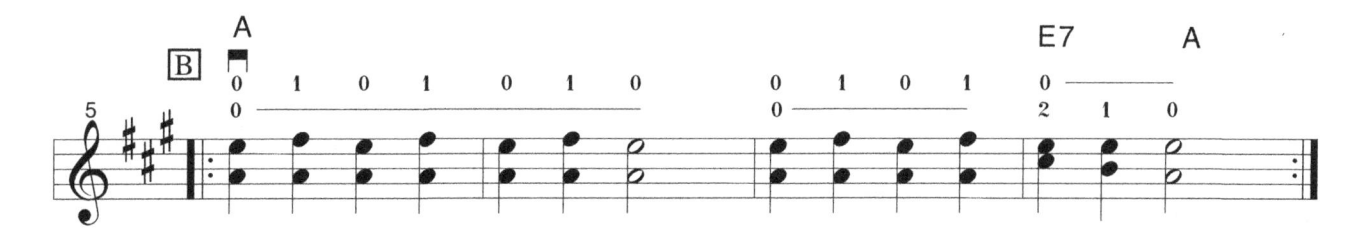

Camptown Races Drone Variation

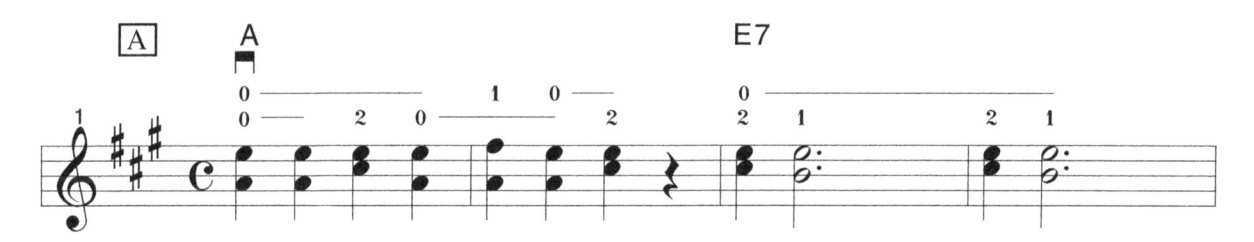

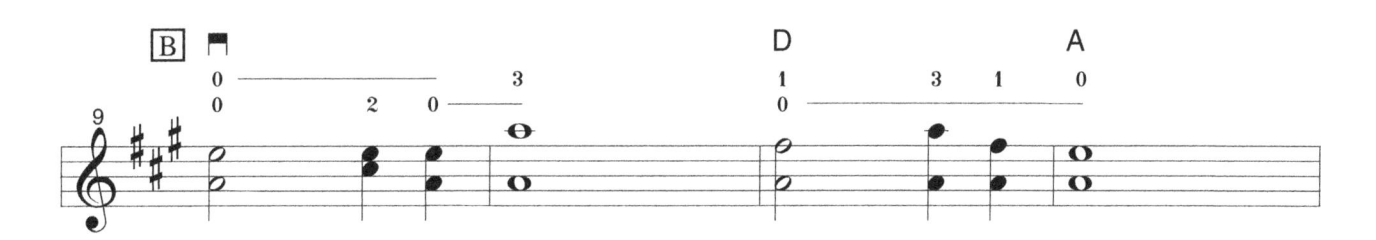

Angelina Baker Drone Variation

Angelina Baker *shows how you can switch drone strings to better complement the chord (third finger D notes on the A string are paired with the open D string).*

Cripple Creek Drone Variation

This version of **Cripple Creek** *demonstrates the use of drones in only part of the melody for variety and to prevent the tune from sounding too heavy.*

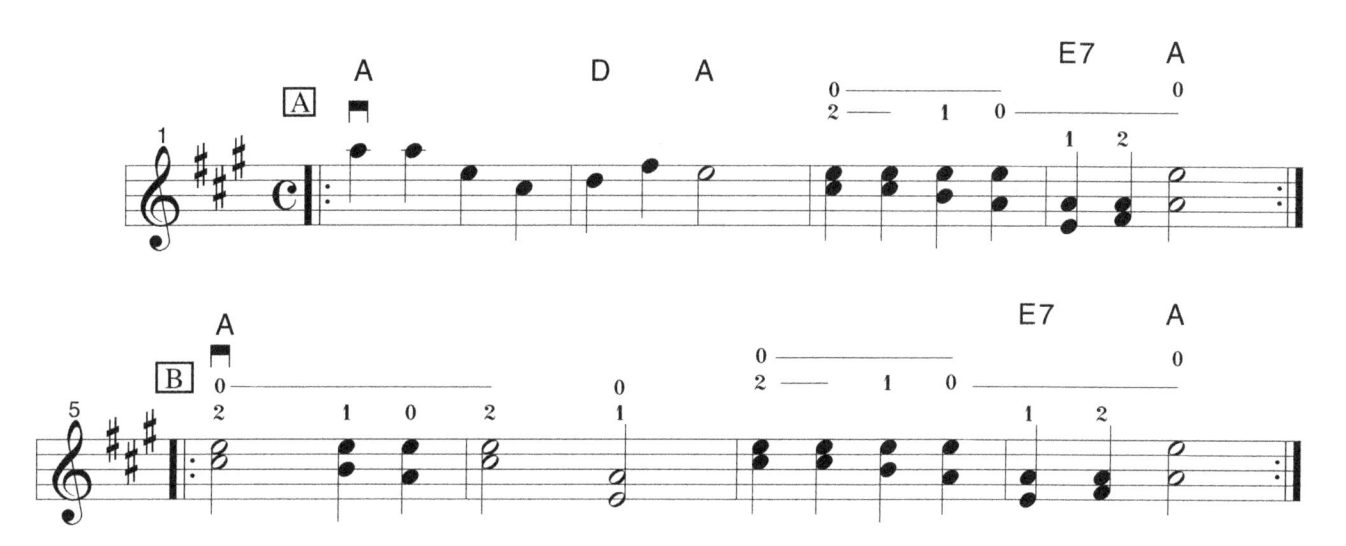

Soldier's Joy Drone Variation

In measure 12, be careful to continue to play the A and E strings and not switch to droning the D string. The E note harmonizes better with the melody than the D string does.

Boil 'em Cabbage Down Drone Variation

In measures 2, 6 and 12 of Boil 'em Cabbage Down, *the best harmony is not an open-string drone, but a double-stop requiring the fingering of both strings.*

Slide Variations

Fiddle players also use the slide or *glissando* to subtly vary the melody. Begin the slide one half-step below the melody note. I have picked the following tunes to demonstrate slide technique, although they can be used to some degree in any of the tunes in this book. Listen to the recording to copy the attack, then explore the use of slides in other tunes in this book. The examples are listed in order of difficulty. They begin with examples of second finger slides, then third finger and finally first finger. Fourth finger slides will be done in *American Fiddle Method Volume 2*.

Boil 'em Cabbage Down Slide Variation

Boil 'em Cabbage Down *demonstrates sliding with the second finger.*

Shortnin' Bread Slide Variation

Shortnin' Bread *shows third finger slides.*

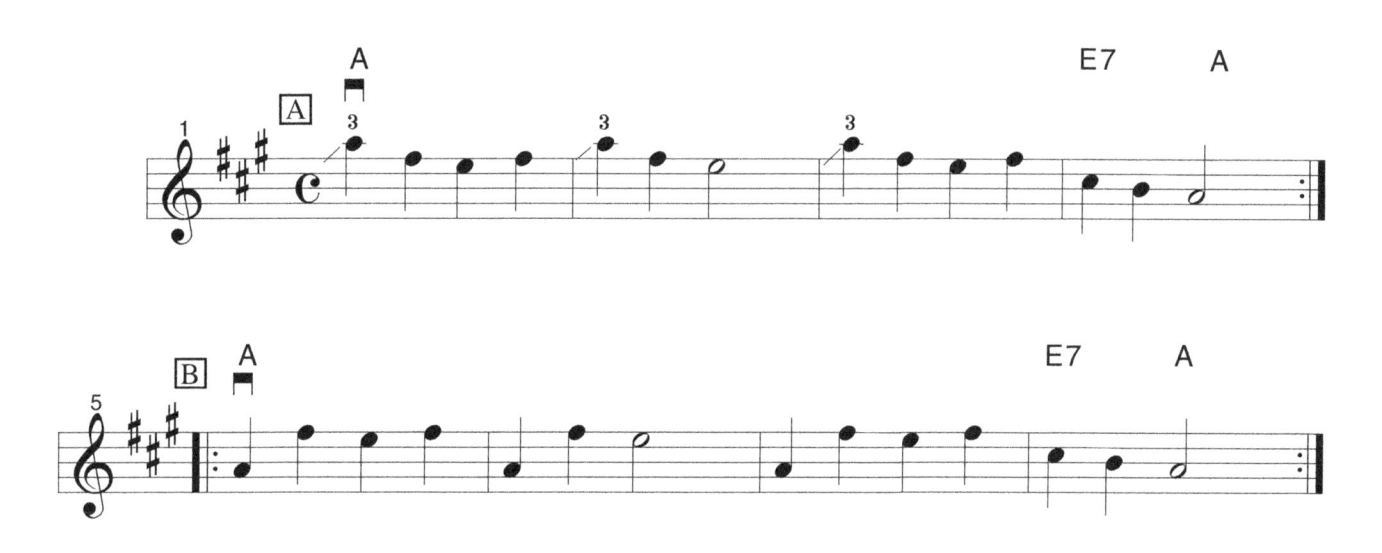

Cripple Creek Slide Variation

Cripple Creek *has both second and third finger slides.*

Cindy Slide Variation

Cindy works the first finger slide.

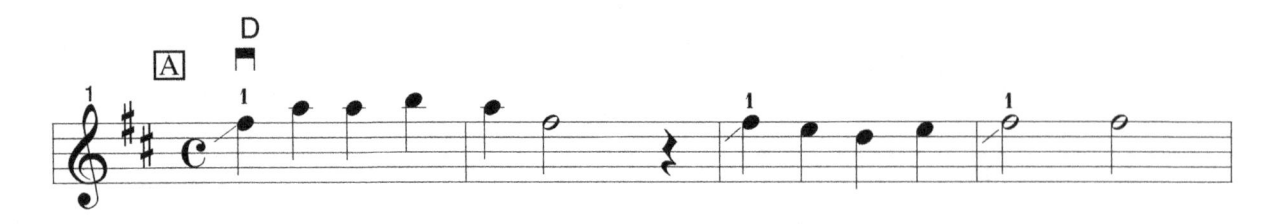

Beginning Backup Fiddle Playing

There are basically two different approaches to ensemble playing in fiddle music: unison and solo playing. Styles such as Appalachian old-time, Irish, New England and French Canadian are traditionally played in a unison style. Fiddles, banjos, mandolins, and accordions all play the melody at the same time while they are accompanied by a bass, guitar, or piano.

However, styles such as bluegrass, cajun, country, blues, and western swing usually feature one instrumentalist at a time. Everyone in the ensemble gets a solo. In this case, when not taking a solo, the fiddle's role changes to backup. This skill requires a basic knowledge of music theory, the fingerboard of the fiddle and the chord order to each of the tunes.

The tunes in the recording that accompanies this book have all been recorded with the fiddle backup in the solo style, even on tunes that are traditionally played in unison. I believe it is important to know the chords to each of the tunes you learn. Then you can jam in the unison style or the solo style. Both styles are challenging and fun.

There are many levels of understanding of backup playing. In later books, we will discuss music theory and more advanced backup techniques, and we'll learn many different double-stop combinations. For now, however, we will keep it simple. First memorize the double-stop for each chord. On the following page are examples for each chord used in this book. Then memorize the chord order for each tune. The chords are written as capital letters above the notation of the tunes in the book. Next play along with the recording and practice taking solos and playing backup. Finally, jam with other musicians.

Notice that all of the chords are played on the lower end of the fiddle's range, using the G, D and A strings. Playing the double-stop in a higher range gets in the way of the soloist. For now, you don't need to concern yourself with the 7th chords, just play the root of each chord.

Bow the double-stops with either a long, smooth bow, or with "chunks." Chunks are played with sharp down-bows on the off-beat. On the recording, I alternate between long bow and chunk-style backup on every tune. Listen to the recording to hear how they are played.

Chord Chart

A or A min chord	E or E min chord	D maj chord

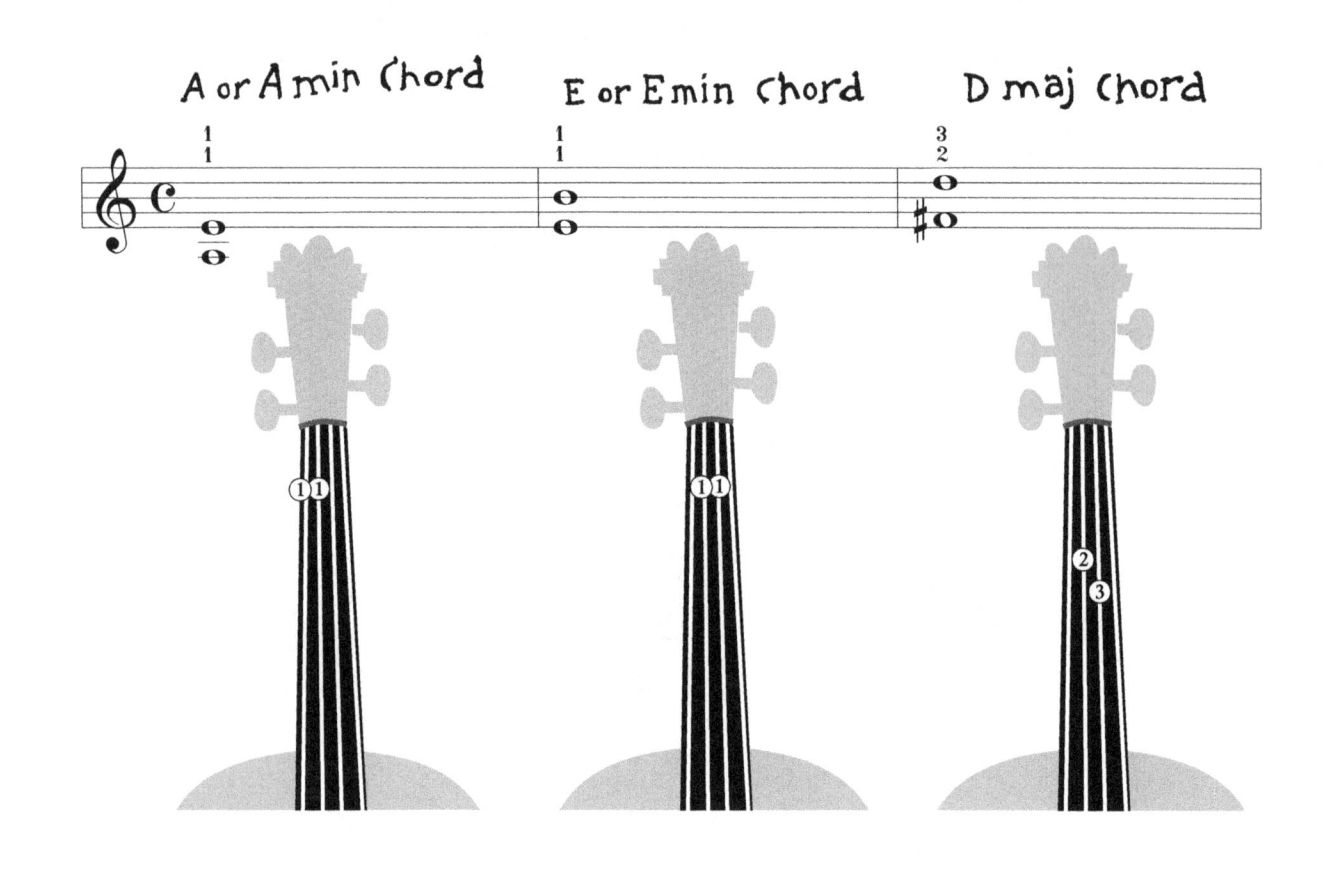

G maj chord	C maj chord	B or B min chord	A or C# min chord

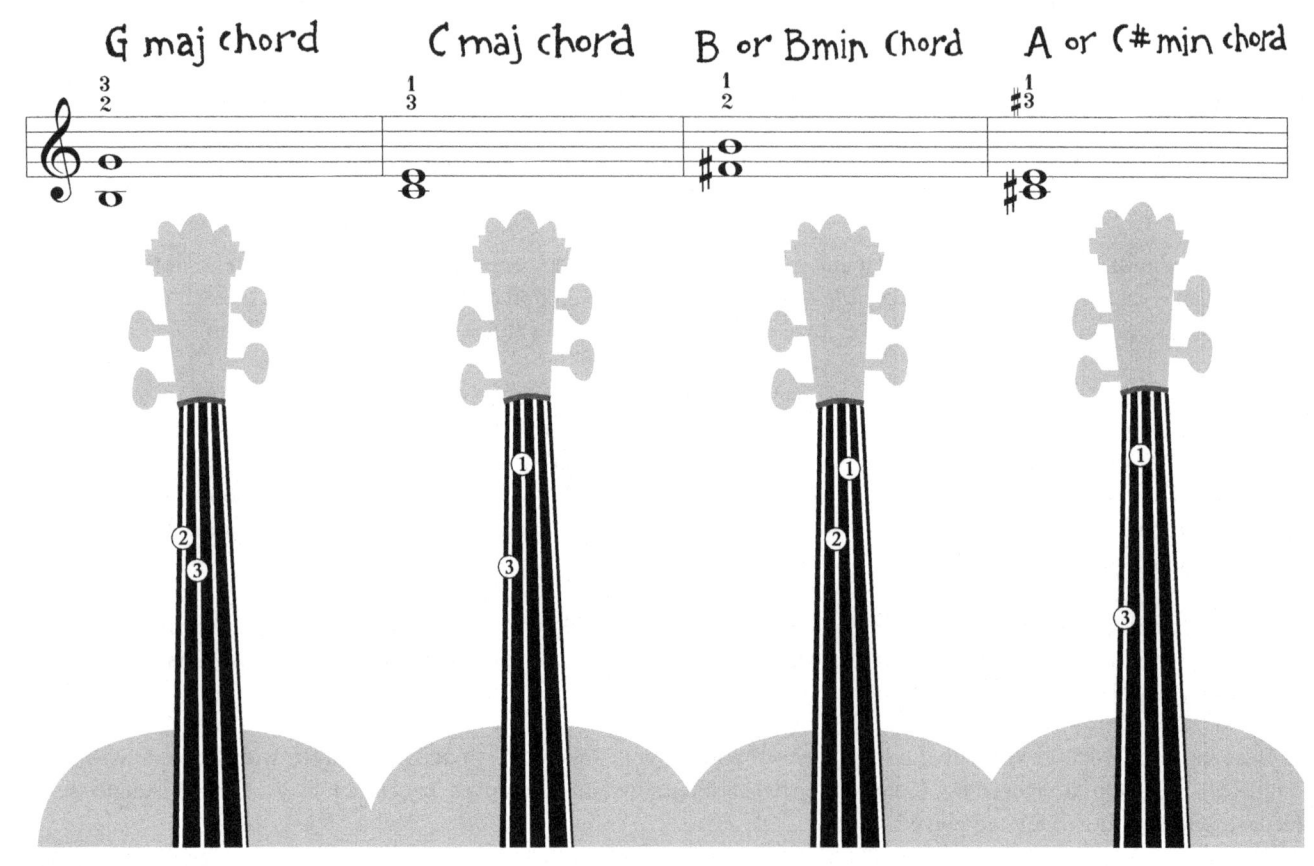

Boil 'em Cabbage Down Long Bow Backup

Here is an example of how you would play backup to Boil 'em Cabbage Down *in the long-bow style. When first finger plays two notes at once, make sure your finger is upright (in the mirror position), and use the tip (not the pad) of your finger to push both strings down evenly.*

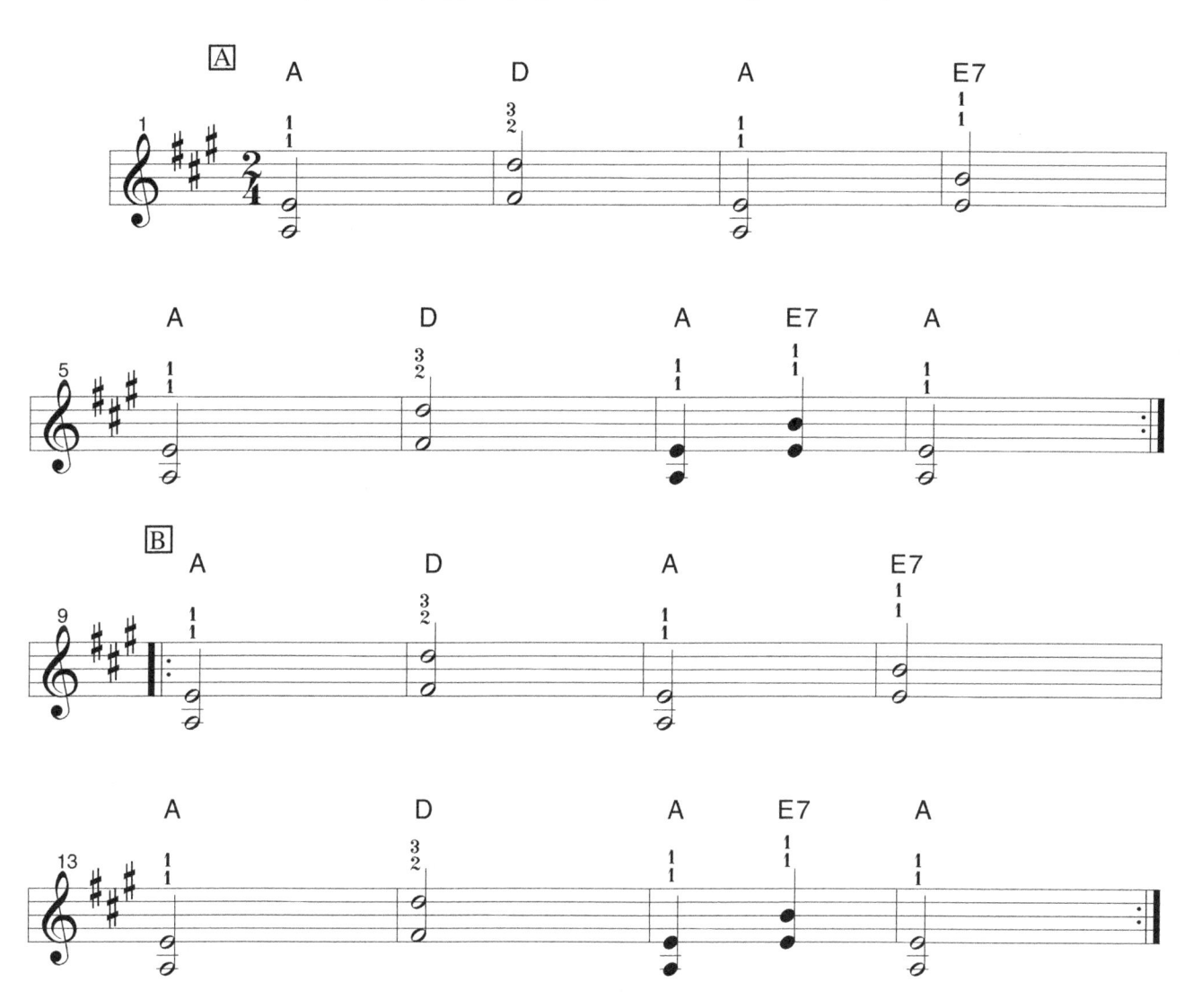

Boil 'em Cabbage Down "Chunk" Backup

Here is the backup to Boil 'em Cabbage Down *in the "chunk" style. A chunk is a cool technique fiddlers use to play the off-beats like the high hat of a drum kit. Keep your wrist and fingers flexible on the bow hold, and drop your bow onto the string making at "tkch" sound. The best way to learn how to chunk is to sit in a jam next to a player who can chunk; watch, listen and learn.*

Country Waltz "Chunk" Backup

In a tune in 3/4 time, like Country Waltz, *you chunk on beats 2 and 3.*

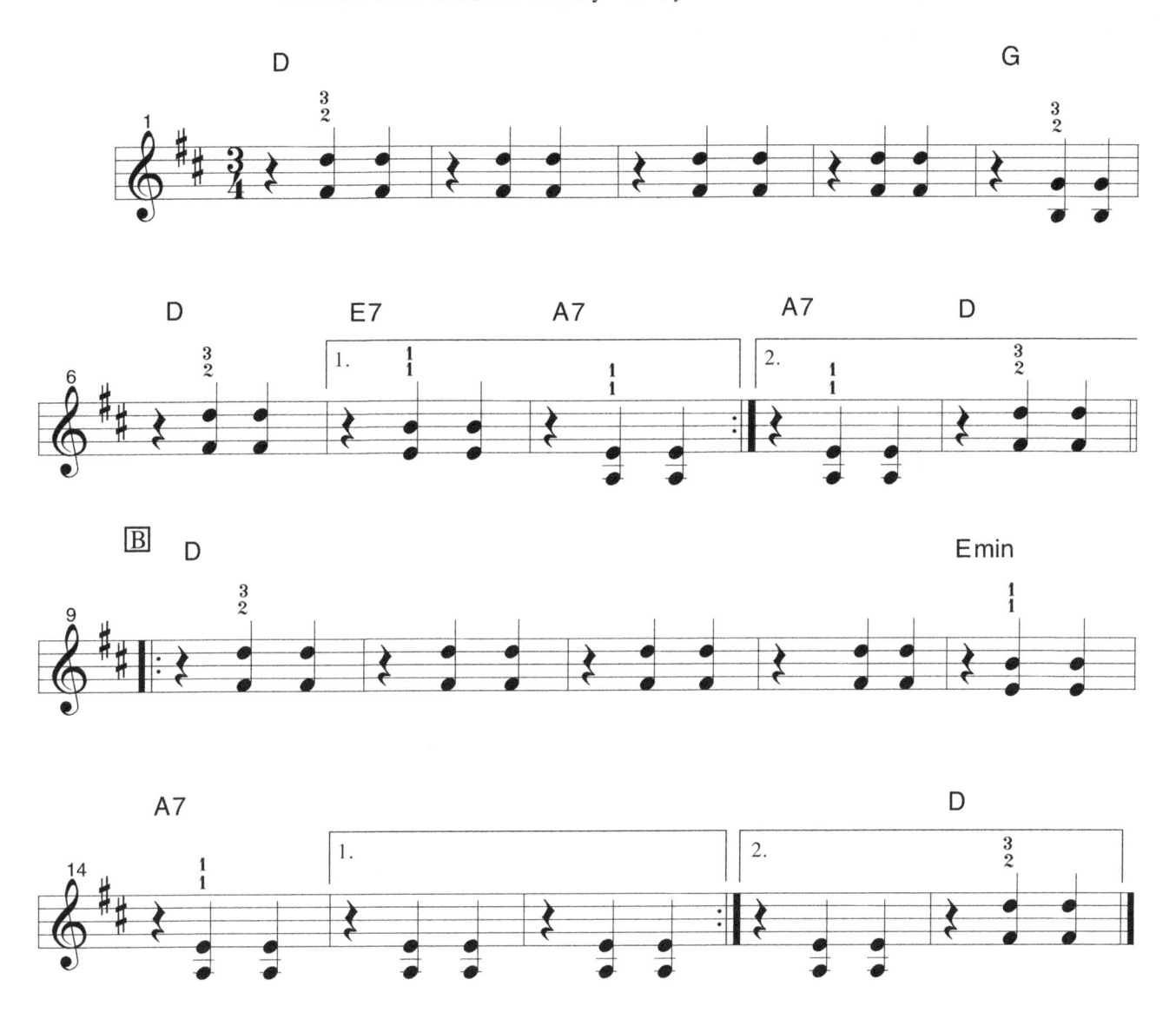

Review Chart

After you can play a tune without mistakes, write down the date and continue down the list. Do another review session a few months later and then one more a few months after that. Don't forget the variations and the chords. If you do a good job reviewing, you'll remember the tunes forever!

		Date	Date	Date
1	Boil 'em Cabbage Down			
2	Shortnin' Bread			
3	Cripple Creek			
4	Camptown Races			
5	Angelina Baker			
6	Buffalo Gals			
7	Cindy			
8	Crawdad Song			
9	Old Joe Clark			
10	Soldier's Joy			
11	Arran Boat Song			
12	Bonaparte's Retreat			
13	Country Waltz			
14	Red Haired Boy			
15	Girl I Left Behind Me			
16	Southwind			
17	Red Wing			
18	Cairo			
19	Turkey in the Straw			
20	Grandfather's Clock			
21	Wise Old Friend			
22	Stinky's Blues			

For the Ensemble Teacher

To make it easy for teachers to use the violin, viola and cello methods together in schools, this chart shows the layout for all three books. The tunes always have the same page number. The chart shows which pieces use high 2nd (H2), low 2nd (L2), high 3rd (H3) or 4th (4) fingers for violin and viola; and "regular" (reg) or forward extension (x4) for cello.

Violas and cellos have the same music as violins to play along on all the violin technique pages (4th finger, low 2nd, high 3rd). Because the key of A requires high 3rd for viola and extensions for cello earlier than for violin, there are some additional technique pages (numbered with an "A") inserted into the viola and cello books to keep the pedagogical sequence logical for viola and cello.

Page #	All Books	Violin	Viola	Cello
6	How to Become a Great Fiddler			
7	Technique	The Parts of a Fiddle	The Parts of a Viola (same as violin)	The Parts of a Cello
8–9	Technique	Bow and Fiddle Position	Viola and Bow Position (same as violin)	Cello and Bow Position
10	Technique	Fingering Position	Fingering Position (same as violin)	Fingering Position
10A			High 3rd Finger (violins and cellos can play along from page 39)	Before and After Rule (for cellos only)
11	Fingering Exercise			
12	Anatomy of a Fiddle Tune			
13	Potato Introductions 1, 2, 3, 4, 5			Cellos also have Potato Harmonics
14	Endings	1, 2, 3, 4 (repeat 2 to play along with viola and cello 2a)	1, 2, 2a, 3 (repeat 3 to play along with violin 4)	1, 2, 2a, 3 (repeat 3 to play along with violin 4)
15	*Boil 'em Cabbage*	H2	H2	reg
16	*Shortnin' Bread*	H2	H2	reg
16A		Play along from page 16	*Shortnin' Bread Adv.* H3	*Shortnin' Bread Adv.* x4
17	*Cripple Creek*	H2	H3 *Cripple Creek Adv.* H3	x4 *Cripple Creek Adv.* x4
18	*Camptown Races*	H2	H3	x4
19	*Angelina Baker*	H2	H2	reg
20	*Buffalo Gals*	H2	H3	x4
21	Technique	4th Finger	4th Finger (For Violas Only) 4th Finger (play along with violins)	Extension Review (play along with violins) Word Finder
22	*Cindy*	H2, 4	H2, 4	reg
23	*Crawdad Song*	H2, 4	H2, 4	reg
24	Technique	Low 2nd Finger	High 3 Quiz (play along with violins)	Extension Quiz (play along with violins)
24A			Low 2nd Finger (For Violas Only)	
25	Technique	Low 2nd Finger (cont.)	Low 2nd Finger (same as violins)	Finger 2 or Finger 3 Quiz (play along with violins)
26	*Old Joe Clark*	L2	H3	x4
27	*Soldier's Joy*	L2	H3, 4	x4
27A		Play along from page 27	*Soldier's Joy Adv.* H3, 4	Play along from page 27
28	*Arran Boat Song*	L2	H2	reg

59

Page #	All Books	Violin	Viola	Cello
29–30	Down-Driven Bowing and Corrective Slurs			
31 "top"	*Bonaparte's Retreat*	H2, 4	H2, 4	reg *Bonapart's Retreat* Advanced 2nd pos
31 "bottom"	*Country Waltz*	L2, 4	H3, 4	x4
32	*Red Haired Boy*	L2	H3, 4	x4
33	*Girl I left Behind Me*	L2	H3	x4
34	*Southwind*	L2, 4	L2, H3	x4
35	Bow Reset & Staccato Slurs			
36	*Red Wing*	L2, 4	L2, 4	reg *Red Wing* Adv. 2nd pos
37	*Cairo*	L2	H3	x4
38	*Turkey in the Straw*	L2, 4	H2	reg
39	Technique	High 3rd Finger	Fingering Review (play along with violins)	Fingering Review (play along with violins) *Grandfather's Clock* Advanced 2nd pos
40	*Grandfather's Clock*	H3, 4	H3, 4	x4
41	*Wise Old Friend*	H3, 4	H3, 4	x4
42–43	*Stinky's Blues*	L2, H3, 4	L2, H3, 4	x4
44	Creating Your Own Variations			
44A		Violins should play along from page 23	*Crawdad Song* Drone H2	*Crawdad Song* Drone reg
45	*Shortnin' Bread* Drone *Camptown Races* Drone	H2 H2	H2 H3	reg x4
46	*Angelina Baker* Drone	H2	H2	reg
46A		Violins should play along from page 22	*Cindy* Drone H2	*Cindy* Drone reg
47	*Cripple Creek* Drone	H2	H3	x4
48	*Soldier's Joy* Drone	L2	H3	x4
49	*Boil 'em Cabbage* Drone	H2	H2	reg
50	*Boil 'em Cabbage* Slide	H2	H2	reg
51	*Shortnin' Bread* Slide *Cripple Creek* Slide	H2 H2	H2 H3	reg x4
52	*Cindy* Slide	H2, 4	H2,4	reg
53	Beginning Backup Playing			
54	Technique	Chord examples	Chord examples	Chord example
55	*Boil 'em Cabbage* Long Bow	H2	H2	reg *Boil 'em Cabbage* Long Bow Bass Line (reg)
55A		Violins should play along from page 15 or page 55	Violas should play along from page 15 or page 55	*Boil 'em Cabbage* Basic Bass Line (reg)
56	*Boil 'em Cabbage* Chunk	H2	H2	reg *Boil 'em Cabbage* Slap off-beats
56A		Violins should play along from page 15 or page 55	Violas should play along from page 15 or page 55	*Boil 'em Cabbage* Bass Line & Slap off-beats (reg)
57	*Country Waltz* Chunk	H2	H2	reg *Country Waltz* Slap off-beat, Bass Line & Slap (reg)
58	Review Chart			

A Guide to Bluegrass Style Arranging

As discussed in the Backup section of the book, bluegrass style jams differ from many other folk style jams in that rather than everyone playing the melody in unison, one person at a time plays a solo on his or her instrument. That means that when not playing a solo, musicians play backup. Below are a couple of examples of how tunes could be arranged. A jam leader can use this as a guide for getting started.

	Fiddle	**Mandolin**	**Banjo**	**Guitar**	**Bass**
1st time	**Intro / Solo**	Chunk	Rolls	Strum	Bass line
2nd time	Chunk	**Solo**	Chunk	Strum	Bass line
3rd time	Long bow	Chunk	**Solo**	Strum	Bass line
4th time	Chunk	Chunk	Rolls	**Solo**	Bass line
5th time	**Solo / ending**	Chunk	Rolls	Strum	Bass line

Here's another possibility:

	Fiddle	**Cello**	**Viola**	**Piano**	**Bass**
1st time	**Intro / Solo**	Long bow	Chunk	Back up	Bass line
2nd time	Chunk	**Solo**	Long bow	Back up	Bass line
3rd time	Long bow	Chunk	**Solo**	Back up	Bass line
4th time	Chunk	Slap	Long bow	**Solo**	Bass line
5th time	**Solo / ending**	**Solo / ending**	**Solo / ending**	Back up	Bass line

And, a possibile arrangement to a song with singing:

Vocal	Fiddle	Cello	Viola	Piano	Bass
	Intro / Solo	Long bow	Chunk	Back up	Bass line
Verse 1	Long bow	Chunk	Long bow	Back up	Bass line
Chorus	Long bow	Chunk	Long bow	Back up	Bass line
	Chunk	**Solo**	Long bow	Back up	Bass line
Verse 2	Long bow	Long bow	Chunk	Back up	Bass line
Chorus	Long bow	Long bow	Chunk	Back up	Bass line
	Long bow	Chunk	**Solo**	Back up	Bass line
Verse 3	Chunk	Chunk	Long bow	Back up	Bass line
Chorus	Chunk	Chunk	Long bow	Back up	Bass line
	Long bow	Chunk	Chunk	**Solo**	Bass line
Verse 4	Long bow	Slap	Long bow	Back up	Bass line
Chorus	Long bow	Slap	Long bow	Back up	Bass line
	Chunk	Long bow	Chunk	Back up	**Solo**
Chorus	Chunk	Long bow	Chunk	Back up	Bass line

Use this chart to make your own arrangement

The publisher gives permission to photocopy this page.

BRIAN WICKLUND'S FiddlePal

Be a FiddlePal!
Books, Videos, Instruction, Fun
www.**fiddlepal**.com

Made in the USA
Monee, IL
22 September 2019